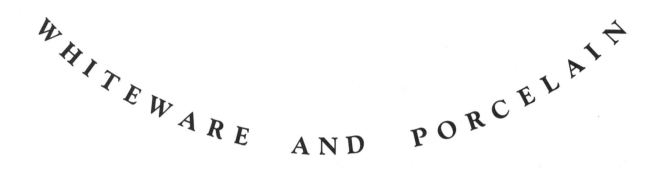

THE DICTIONARY

of

AMERICAN POTTERY MARKS

WHITEWARE AND PORCELAIN

BY

C. GERALD DeBOLT

THE FIRST BOOK OF ITS KIND IN OVER EIGHTY YEARS

CHARLES E. TUTTLE COMPANY
Rutland, Vermont & Tokyo, Japan

REPRESENTATIVES:
  British Isles & Continental Europe:
    Simon & Schuster International Group, London
  Australasia:
    Bookwise International
    1 Jeanes Street, Beverly, 5009, South Australia

Published by the Charles E. Tuttle Company, Inc.
of Rutland, Vermont & Tokyo, Japan
with editorial offices at
Suido 1-chome, 2-6, Bunkyo-ku, Tokyo

Library of Congress Catalog Number: 88-50739

International Standard Book Number: 0-8048-7027-6

First Printing — 1988

Printed in USA

PREFACE

Although early American whiteware is not yet a major factor in the field of antique collecting, I believe this is soon to change. I hope this book will help to bring about that change.

Generally, the American whiteware industry of the nineteenth century lagged behind its British counterpart. This notwithstanding, there is a considerable amount of American ware that compares to the best made in England. By the 1890s America was producing much excellent whiteware. Whatever the quality, early American whiteware deserves consideration by the serious antique collector.

There are a number of reasons why early American whiteware has the potential for becoming an important collectible. First, there is enough of it around to make it possible to collect, yet it is scarce enough to make the searching for it a bit of a challenge. Second, many of the early pieces qualify as genuine antiques, now being 100 or more years old. There is a small, but not yet rare, quantity of it dating from the 1870s. Pieces from the 1880s, and especially the 1890s, are fairly abundant. Pieces from the early years of the 1900s are also reasonably available.

A third factor making early American whiteware attractive to collectors is the price. Dealers and collectors do not yet know very much about American whiteware. They are usually unaware of the age of much old and even rare early ware. Consequently, there is an excellent chance you can find some really nice old pieces for very reasonable prices. This is destined to change. Recent research and resultant publications will inevitably attract the attention of the general antique collecting public. That may well cause prices to soar. Now is the time to collect early American whiteware.

Another factor is the diversity of styling. Comparable British whiteware usually followed tried and true conventional styles. They tend to be tasteful but predictable. With American whiteware, the opposite is often true. There is considerable variety and innovation. Some styling is awfully good; some is merely awful! Seldom is it boring, and that is the fun of it.

A final consideration for the prospective collector is that reproductions are not and probably will not become a serious problem. Only if prices become excessive is the problem likely to appear. Even then, convincing reproductions will be difficult to make.

ACKNOWLEDGMENTS

First, I would like to thank the friends and family members who have supported me through the ups and downs of the many months of researching and writing of this book.

Second, I would like to recognize the many hundreds of antique dealers throughout the eastern United States who have helped me in one way or another.

Finally, I would like to thank the following for giving me special help: the Jamisons of Corning, N.Y.; Marie Reiter of Pittsburgh, Pa.; Roma and Rhonda Holloway, also of Pittsburgh, Pa.; Jane Crane, Uniontown, Pa.; Faith Fearer, Uniontown, Pa.; the staff of the Uniontown Public Library, Uniontown, Pa.; Bud Franks of the Fayette Printing Co., Uniontown, Pa.; Ronald L. Michael, editor of the Society of Historical Archaeology, California University, California, Pa.; Florence Corder and Ethel Fox of New Geneva, Pa.; Lee and Adam Sedlock Antiques, R.D.#2, Perryopolis, Pa.; Hessie Lint, South Connellsville, Pa.; Leonard A. Elby, Connellsville, Pa.; Joanna Miller and Bill Maust of the Casselman Antiques, Grantsville, Md.; Joyce Miller, Bridgewater, Va.; and Rocky and the dealers of Rocky's Antique Mall, Rt. 11, north of Staunton, Va.

TABLE OF CONTENTS

THE PURPOSE AND PROPER USE OF THIS BOOK

The purpose of this book is to help identify the manufacturer, the place of manufacture, and the approximate age of old American whiteware or porcelain from its mark, if, indeed, it has a mark.

What Is Whiteware?

Whiteware is any pottery that has been refined to the extent that, in its natural state, it is white or nearly white. It includes all pottery from cream-colored ware (Queen's Ware) to porcelain. Porcelain is the most highly refined whiteware. Whiteware is usually associated with dinnerware; however, its uses included almost anything — from spittoons to hair receivers.

This book is designed to help the serious collector of old American whiteware as well as the novice trying to identify that fancy old Victorian tureen aunt Alice gave you before she moved to her condo in Florida. A thoughtfully and carefully constructed index is the key to this book. It is designed to help you identify a mark with minimum information and effort. To save time and needless frustration, you should read the following seven steps before attempting to use the index.

STEP I. COUNTRY OF MANUFACTURE

The first thing to look for on a mark is the name of a foreign country, usually below the mark — infrequently above. If it is marked England, France, Germany, etc., then it is obviously not made in the U.S.A. Nippon or Silesia may not be so easy. English pottery marks often include a regional mark. Staffordshire is the best known. These marks are included in the index. Also, the index includes company names, initials, and words commonly found on foreign marks and identifies the country of manufacture. Many, particularly old, European marks include no words. The index is designed to help you identify these marks as being of foreign origin.

If you now have concluded that your mark is not foreign, go on to STEP II.

STEP II. COMPANY NAME OR INITIALS

The name of a company or its initials found anywhere on a mark often makes the identification of an item very easy. If the mark has what appears to be a company name, simply look it up in the book's alphabetical listing of American companies and their marks. If it is not there, then look for it in the index. There are two reasons for this. First, the company may not have started until the 1930s or later. Second, what appears to be a company name may in fact not be. For example, Mellor & Co. on a mark actually indicates the Cook Pottery Co. There are various reasons for this. In any case remember to look for these "company names" in the index.

All company initials, or apparent company initials, are listed in the index and should be easy to find. If you're certain you're reading the initials correctly and they are not listed in the index, then that company is probably a foreign one. The index includes many foreign company names and initials, particularly from the 1800s and early 1900s; however, I am sure many later companies have been overlooked.

A warning about initials on marks:

Be very careful about ascribing a mark that consists *only* of initials to any particular company. C. Jordan Thorn, who wrote a marks book in the 1940s, erroneously attributed an

S.P.Co. mark to the Southern Porcelain Co. Barber in his 1904 marks book said that the only mark he could find for this old company was the one listed in this book. See p. 66. This was marked on telegraph insulators! He *believed* that other items may have been so marked. Southern Porcelain Co. products are very rare. If you have an item marked only S.P. Co. it was made by the Steubenville Pottery Co. or, possibly, the Sebring Pottery Co. Again, be very careful about ascribing any mark that consists only of initials to any particular company. Only do so if it was listed by Barber or if you have other *irrefutable* evidence!

If a mark has no company name or initials, or if the name or initials are not legible, go on to step III.

STEP III. AN IDENTIFYING WORD

If a mark has no company name or initials or if same is not legible, look for any identifying words. On American marks such words usually indicate a pattern, a shape, .or a special product of that company. Don't use such words as semi-porcelain, ironstone china, semi-vitreous, white granite, warranted, etc. Such terms are very commonly used on American marks (similar terms on English marks) and are generally useless for identifying marks. However, if such a term is the *only* word or words on a mark, it will be listed in the index — if it's an American mark.

If there are no identifying words on a mark or if they are not legible, go on to STEP IV.

STEP IV. DESCRIBING THE MARK

If you can't see or make out any words or initials on a mark, pick out some obvious feature that might generally describe it.

Examples might be a globe, a wreath, a moon or crescent, an eagle, a bird (if it doesn't look like an eagle), a lion, *two* lions, a horse, *two* horses, a lion and a unicorn (actually the British Coat of Arms), and many more. Note that if two different animals are on a mark the one on the left will be listed first in the index.

If the most distinguishing feature about a mark is its shape — a square, a diamond, a rectangle, etc., — look that shape up in the index. However, *a circle is not listed*; it is so commonly used that its inclusion would confuse the index. There is not a single American mark that needs to be described as a circle.

The first four steps are general in nature; the next three deal with specific categories of marks.

STEP V. THE BRITISH (ENGLISH) COAT OF ARMS

The British Coat of Arms mark consists of a lion, a central shield with a crown on top, and a unicorn. One variant has a second lion instead of the unicorn. You may be surprised that the British Coat of Arms was used rather frequently to mark early American wares. It was done with the intent of making the product appear to be of British origin. The general public believed British-made wares were superior to American-made wares. Often they were. To help insure sales, newly formed companies and older companies having financial troubles would resort to marking with the British Arms. Barber believed the first use of the Arms mark in America was by Rouse & Turner c.1850 at the Jersey City Pottery. Barber listed about 50 different British Arms marks used by American companies, some using two or more variations. Fortunately, most have company names, initials, or some identifying words to tell them apart. However, there are 32 British Arms marks (including a two-lion variant) that are difficult to distinguish. These marks are shown on pages 99 to 105.

STEP VI. MONOGRAMS

If at all possible, try to identify a mark without using monograms. The Victorians of the late 1800s loved monograms, seemingly the more complicated the better. Many pottery marks incorporate monograms in one way or another. Some are large and obvious; others are so tiny, as on the shield of a British Arms mark, that it takes a magnifying glass to see them. Some are fairly easy to decipher. Others are very difficult, particularly regarding the intended order of the letters. If you can identify the order of the letters in a monogram, you will find them in the index. If you can't decipher a monogram,

use something else to identify the mark. For example: one mark of the East Palestine Pottery Co. is just the company monogram inside a wreath with no words. In this case, look under the word "wreath" in the index. Here it is listed: a wreath (with E.P.P. Co. monogram inside).

In some instances a monogram may make up the entire mark, or the monogram has a nondescript background. If you have such a mark and you can't decipher its monogram, see pages 109 to 112.

STEP VII. NONDESCRIPT MARKS

Finally, if you have a mark that is an unfathomable monogram or otherwise defies description, see pages 109-112. Use these pages only as a last resort.

WHAT IS EARLY AMERICAN WHITEWARE?

Prior to the 1980s, books dealing with American whiteware marks dealt primarily with the period before 1900. They did not try to extend their coverage beyond that of Edwin A. Barber's *Marks of American Potters* published in 1904. This book extends that coverage to c.1930. Any whiteware made before 1920 can be considered early. This is an historical, not an arbitrary, definition. The main event for bringing about the division was World War I, for America that being 1917-1918. The war changed America profoundly, and that change is reflected in the United States' pottery industry. No longer would we be content to look back to Europe. A new American patriotism brought about a pride in things made in the U.S.A. American companies, using mass-production techniques, were already gearing up to keep the domestic whiteware markets that the dislocations of war had denied their European counterparts.

The 1920s was a period of transition. For many older companies that did not modernize, the 1920s proved difficult, culminating in total collapse with the coming of the Great Depression. For a small number of progressive companies, the 1920s was the springboard to the future. The next 30 years would be the era of American dominance in the domestic whiteware industry. This dominance would even extent, albeit to a lesser degree, to fine porcelain. The granting to the Lenox Co. in 1917 the right to supply dinner service for the White House was a major event in the industry. This was the first time this honor had gone to an American company. No longer would our country's industry take a back seat to the European industry.

In summary:

Prior to the 1920s

1. The American public generally favored European whiteware, particularly fine porcelain.

2. The industry often used marks that concealed their U.S. identity.

3. The industry looked to Europe for innovation.

4. The industry was not geared for mass-production.

After the 1920s

1. Those U.S. companies that retooled for mass-production generally prospered.

2. Americans began to look to their own countrymen for innovation.

3. MADE IN U.S.A. was proudly proclaimed on marks.

HOW TO RECOGNIZE EARLY AMERICAN WHITEWARE AND ITS MARKS

I. Distinguishing Characteristics of Early American Whiteware*

It is a good idea to learn something about what early American whiteware looks like before you begin searching for early American marks. While not necessary for the using of this book, a little knowledge about early whiteware will save you some time and effort. Some study of books on the subject and a few visits to antique shops or shows will help you develop a sense of what to look for. Once you have developed a sense for the "Victorian" or "turn-of-the-century" look, you might want to try determining if the ware is American or imported. While early American potters often copied European styles, there are differences. Some are subtle and take considerable experience to detect.

Some differences came about because of the technical problems encountered by the early American potters. Since most Americans in the early industry were English themselves, some with prior experience in the English industry or they hired English experts to help get them started, they naturally attempted to make their whiteware as it had been made in England. Using American clays and other raw materials, however, caused English methods to not always work as planned. Some companies failed completely. Others had limited success. Even then, the resulting whiteware was often not as good as its English counterpart. One example of this is the problem of crazing. Crazing is a fine web of tiny cracks in the glaze of whiteware caused by the improper matching of the glaze to the whiteware body below. Experience had helped the English to minimize the problem. However, English solutions to the problem often failed when dealing with American raw materials. While not all early American whiteware is subject to crazing, much of it is. Imported European wares of this same period will generally not have crazing. These wares are often porcelain or fairly comparable to porcelain. Due to their vitrified state these wares will not have crazing. Because of the materials and the intensity of the heat used in firing, porcelain is vitrified (glass-like) and, therefore, translucent. English whiteware from the early and middle 1800s, however, is subject to crazing as is some later English Staffordshire ware. The crazing on British Staffordshire tends to be delicate with the lines smaller and closer together than on American whiteware.

A Word of Warning:

1. Some early (before 1920) American whiteware shows no crazing.

2. Some late (after 1920) American whiteware does show crazing.

II. Distinguishing Early American Marks from Foreign Marks

A. Foreign Marks in General

The year 1891 is important when discussing foreign marks. The McKinley Tariff Act required that from 1891 on, all wares imported into the United States had to have the country of origin marked on them. With the exception of England, the vast majority of whiteware imported before the 1950s came into the U.S. during the late 1800s and early 1900s. As a result, nearly all early wares from foreign countries, except England, will have the country name as part of its mark. That name, however, may not be the modern or English (language) version. Also, some country marks are really regional

---

* I consider the 1920s a period of transition. The 1920s could be classified early or later.

5

or provincial marks. These various names are listed in the index. In any case, most early foreign whiteware imports, except those from England, will be a hard, translucent porcelain that is not likely to be confused with early American whiteware.

The date 1891 is not always as important as it might seem. Items made to be sold within a particular foreign country, not for export to the United States, did not need the country's name on the mark. Now, many years later, by any number of means, these items can have found their way into the United States. This is particularly true regarding whiteware made in England. Britain had a vast empire with colonies all over the world, including Canada. British wares sent to Canada could easily find their way to the U.S. These wares would not necessarily have England on their marks. Also, vast amounts of British whiteware were imported into the U.S. before 1891. Very little of this was marked with the word "England."

Some much later foreign wares, usually imported into the United States after WWII, were and are marked with paper labels containing the name of the country of origin. See p. 9 for more on this fairly recent problem.

In conclusion:

1. Most foreign whiteware found in the United States today that has a country of origin as part of its mark was made after 1891.

2. However, it *can't* be said that the lack of the country of origin on the mark indicates an American item or a foreign item made before 1891.

B. British Marks

Large amounts of British whiteware were imported into the United States in the 1800s. Most of that imported before 1891 will not have England on the mark. The following information will help you identify British whiteware and its marks.

1. This book's index has a fairly comprehensive listing of company names, initials, regions, cities and towns, etc., found on English marks.

2. In addition to the index, the following general rules for British marks will be helpful.

a. British marks of the 1800s tend to be complex. The elaborate cartouches used by early Staffordshire potters are particularly distinctive:

Nothing like this was used on American whiteware.

b. The use of the Staffordshire knot:

This device was never used on early American marks. In fact, I have never seen an American mark from any period that incorporated the Staffordshire knot.*

The Staffordshire knot was used alone or incorporated into a more complex mark. When used alone, the Staffordshire knot often had letters in the open spaces of the knot representing the initials of the company. Either the left or the middle initial will be the first letter of the company's initials. Usually it is the left one.

---

* I have seen one nearly undetectable exception to this.

c. English town and city names used on marks:

The names of towns and cities are often used on British marks. All of these names are listed in the index. Most of these towns are located in the Staffordshire district of England and may well not be familiar to Americans not well-versed in Staffordshire whiteware. Often the initial of the town was used in conjunction with the company's initials. Often the mark had the town initial alone under the company's initials. If the letter is an "L" it can cause confusion with French Limoges porcelain since some Limoges was marked in a similar way. However, Limoges ware will be translucent porcelain; the English ware will usually be simple opaque whiteware.

A. B. C.
L

d. The use of Ltd. (for Limited):

The use of Ltd. is distinctive to British marks. However, for some reason, one American company, the Chester Pottery Co., did use Ltd. on its marks. See no. 44 on p. 22. Ltd. really had no meaning in this country. All other marks using Ltd. will be British.

e. The British Royal Coat of Arms:

Both American and British companies used this to mark whiteware. See pp. 99 to 105.

f. Initials and Monograms:

Initials are frequently used on British marks and often they are the only thing you can use to distinguish the mark. Those used in the 19th century are often in an elaborate script difficult to read. J's look like I's. Many other letters are hard to make out. This is almost never true with American marks. However, complex monograms were used in both countries. American monograms are discussed elsewhere in this book. See p. 3.

g. Other points about British marks:

(1) Lions, not just as a part of the Royal Coat of Arms, are common on British marks but are fairly rare on American marks.

(2) Crowns, though used by some American companies, are far more common on British marks, particularly after WWI.

(3) BONE CHINA is often used on later English marks; I don't think the term was ever used on American marks.*

(4) The eagle, common on American marks, is rare on British marks. When used on British marks, the eagles are usually copied from eagles found on American coins of the period.

(5) TRADE MARK is far more frequently used on British marks than on American marks.

(6) Some British marks included the word "England" for 10 or more years before 1891.

III. How to Tell an Early American Mark from a Late American Mark:

A. A Barber Mark

In 1904 Edwin AtLee Barber published his *Marks of American Potters*. This book remains an important research tool today. An item that has a mark shown in Barber's book can be said to be irrefutably an early piece. For those companies that continued production well past the 1920s, these early Barber marks are sometimes the only ones

---

* Oxford Bone China introduced by Lenox in 1962 is an exception.

that can be considered unquestionably early. In this book I often refer to a Barber mark as a pre-1904 mark; however, a mark found in Barber's book that was in current use in 1904 could have been used for some time after that. Seldom were they used beyond c.1910. The Edwin M. Knowles vase mark was a major exception. In any case, nearly all the companies listed in Barber's book had ceased production by the time of the Great Depression. Many had ceased production long before that.

B. Characteristics That Early (before 1920)* Marks Will *Not* Have:

1. Early marks will not include U.S.A. or MADE IN U.S.A.

There are a few exceptions to this. Barber listed a few marks with U.S.A. added to the location of manufacture. For example: East Liverpool, Ohio, U.S.A. Only two Barber marks had USA set apart as commonly found on later marks. These were for the East Liverpool Potteries Co. and the Thomas China Co. of Lisbon, Ohio. With these and perhaps a few other exceptions, USA found on a mark will indicate it was from the 1920s or later.

2. An early mark will not say 18 or 22 karat gold, etc. This practice seems to have first started in the late 1920s.

3. Early marks will almost never have numbers or a combination of numbers and letters under the mark. Except for the Homer Laughlin Co. that began the practice in 1901, the Buffalo Pottery, the Edwin M. Knowles China Co., and a few other companies, this form of marking was not done until the 1920s.

4. Early marks will never say BY and the company name. For example: Ivory Porc. *by* Sebring (the Sebring Pottery Co.). This type of mark indicates some special pattern or new whiteware (Ivory Porc. in this case)

made BY a particular company (Sebring in this case). Early marks were never so designed; however, a few did use MADE BY and the company's name. Even this was very rare.

5. Early marks will never say FINE CHINA. Just as BONE CHINA is a late term on British marks, FINE CHINA is a late term used on American marks. It was probably not used until after World War II. FINE CHINA is also found on "fake" marks used on modern Asian imports. See page 9.

6. The name Russel Wright appears on whiteware made in the 1940s and 1950s.

C. Characteristics That Early (before 1920) Marks Will Include:

1. A British Royal Coat of Arms. See pages 99 to 105.

2. Monograms — some quite complex. See pp. 109 to 112 for some monogram marks that are difficult to identify.

3. Fancy "Victorian gingerbread" decoration — this is particularly true of late 19th century marks.

4. Garter marks:

These are similar to British garter marks. American garter marks date from the 1870s to c.1902.

5. Plain marks with company initials:

E.L.P.Co.　　　N.C.Co.　　ADMIRAL
WACO CHINA　　 E.L.O.　　 V.P.Co.

KT&K　 C.P.Co.
CHINA　 ROYAL

These plain marks were used all through the early years to at least c.1920. They seem to have been used most commonly in the first decade of the twentieth century. Marks used in the 1920s were usually simple, but this particular style was infrequently used.

---

* Depending on criteria used, the 1920s could be considered early or not. It was really a transition period.

IV. Fake Marks:

Fake marks are not yet a problem for collectors of early American whiteware. First, these marks are still generally unknown to the collecting public; therefore, reproducing them would be meaningless. Second, early American whiteware seldom commands a monetary premium meriting the reproduction of marks. Third, since much early American whiteware has no marks, a fake mark stamped on an old piece, if at all suspect, might actually lower its value. The potential buyer might now believe the whiteware itself is a reproduction.

The aforementioned not withstanding, I have recently come across some Victorian-looking whiteware complete with old-style marks. Both the whiteware and the marks were new. The marks were not reproductions of old marks, just marks made in an early style. However, it must be kept in mind that when or if early whiteware takes its place with other American antiques, reproductions are sure to follow.

The real problem with fake marks is late American whiteware made after World War II. Japan and other Asian nations produced and continue to produce whiteware with paper labels marked Japan, etc. Once these paper labels are removed, confusion will reign. Some of these wares have no other marks. Other have marks made to simulate American or European marks. I have a plate marked NORCREST FINE CHINA. It also has a paper label with JAPAN on it. Once the paper label is removed there will be no indication as to the country of origin. Many of these imports use the term FINE CHINA. This term is also quite common on the marks of late American whiteware made after World War II. Some of the imported wares are of good quality, others are not. These products are not likely to be confused with early American whiteware, but they are going to cause problems for collectors in the future.

V. Unmarked Ware

Perhaps a book dealing with marks should not discuss unmarked ware; however, since much early American whiteware was not marked, I feel a few points are in order. Only those with considerable experience should try to determine if an unmarked piece is early American. Unmarked items come from all periods from the earliest whiteware made in this country to ware made today. Some will be imports, even modern imports. Imported ware with the country name on just a paper label and no other mark will become unmarked whiteware once the label is removed. American dinnerware sold in sets from at least the 1920s onward that were marked will frequently have some items in the set that will not be marked. Once that item is separated from the rest, it becomes just another unmarked piece of whiteware. It is fine to collect unmarked, apparently early whiteware. The price is often right. However, collect for aesthetic pleasure, not for investment potential.

PRINCIPAL AMERICAN MARKS

1. Acme Pottery (Porcelain) Co.   1903-1905
   Crooksville, Ohio

2. Akron China Co.   1894-1908
   Akron, Ohio

 See p. 101.

3. Akron Queensware Co.   1890-1894
   Akron, Ohio

4. Albright China Co.   1910-c.1930
   Carrollton, Ohio

   Their mark includes ALBRIGHT CHINA

5. Alliance Vitreous China Co.   c.1900-c.1929
   Alliance, Ohio

(c.1920)

6. American Art China Works   1891-c.1899
   (Rittenhouse, Evans & Co.)
   Trenton, N.J.

They made a thin, translucent, belleek type of china.

R.E. & Co. stands for Rittenhouse, Evans & Co.

7. American China Co.   1897-c.1910
   Toronto, Ohio

The first four marks are Barber (pre-1904) marks.

Eugenia

Biltmore

   (c.1905-1910)

See p. 97 for more about this mark.

8. American Crockery Co.   1876-1890s
   Trenton, N.J.

(c.1880)

(c.1890)

AMERICAN CHINA
A.C.CO

9. American Porcelain Manufacturing Co.   1854-1857
   Gloucester, N.J.

A.P.M.Cº

10. American Pottery Co. See Jersey City Pottery on p. 38.

11. American Pottery Works East Liverpool, Ohio and Sebring, Ohio
(Sebring Pottery Co.) (1887-c.1902) (c.1902-c.1940)

The earliest mark was a British Coat of Arms with STONE CHINA and SEBRING BROS. & CO. under the mark. This was used before 1890.

(c.1895-c.1905) (c.1895-c.1905) (c.1895-c.1905)

(c.1900-c.1905) (c.1895)

The mark at left is from Gates and Ormerod. They date it 1895.
See acknowledgment below.*

(after 1904) (c.1905-c.1915)

I found this KOKUS CHINA mark on a bowl with a "modern" decalcomania decoration. This type of decal was seldom used in America before 1900.

(c.1905-c.1915) (c.1910-c.1920) (c.1915-c.1925)

Sebring's IVORY PORCELAIN dates from the mid-1920s to the 1930s. Their JADE WARE is from about the same period.

* This is one of 44 marks reprinted from *Historical Archaeology* Vol. 16, Numbers 1 & 2, p.233 (1982) by permission of the Society for Historical Archaeology, P.O. Box 231033, Pleasant Hill, CA 94523-1033.

12. Anchor Pottery Co.   1894-mid-1920s
    Trenton, N.J.

      J.E. Norris founded the company. His initials can be found on marks used before and after 1904.

      The first 8 marks are Barber (pre-1904) marks.

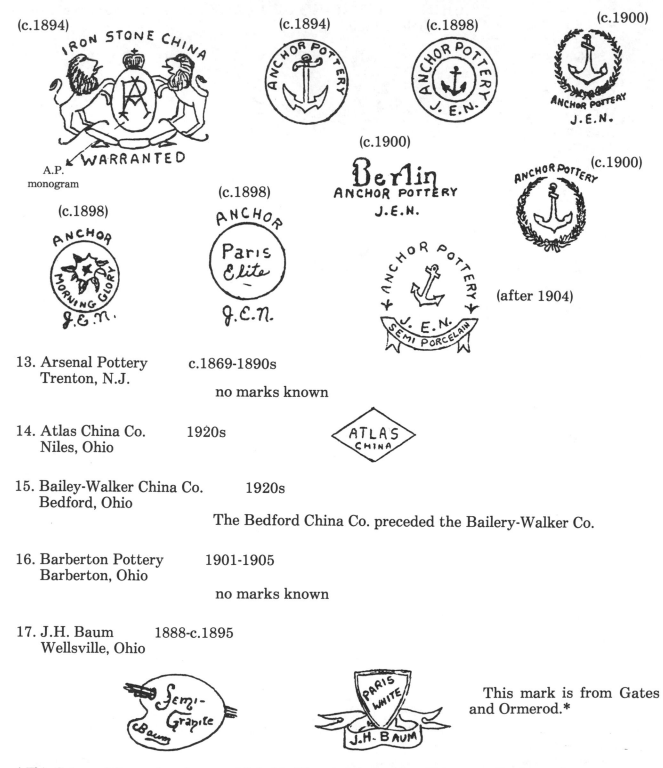

13. Arsenal Pottery   c.1869-1890s
    Trenton, N.J.

      no marks known

14. Atlas China Co.   1920s
    Niles, Ohio

15. Bailey-Walker China Co.   1920s
    Bedford, Ohio

      The Bedford China Co. preceded the Bailery-Walker Co.

16. Barberton Pottery   1901-1905
    Barberton, Ohio

      no marks known

17. J.H. Baum   1888-c.1895
    Wellsville, Ohio

      This mark is from Gates and Ormerod.*

* This Gates and Ormerod mark was published in *Historical Archaeology* Volume 16, Numbers 1 & 2, p.14.

18. L.B. Beerbower & Co.   1879-c.1900
    Elizabeth, N.J.

19. Beerbower & Griffin   1877-1879
    Phoenix Pottery
    Phoenixville, Pa.

   ARMS OF PENNSYLVANIA

20. Bell Pottery Co.   1888-c.1904
    Findlay, Ohio

B. P. Co.
——
F. O.

THE BELL POTTERY CO.
FINDLAY, OHIO

BELL CHINA
B. P. Co.
Findlay, Ohio

21. Edwin Bennett Pottery Co.   1846-1930s
    Baltimore, Md.

(1848-1856)

(1875)

B & W. BENNETT
CANTON AVENUE
BALTIMORE MD.

E. B
STONE CHINA

(1880)

(1884)

21. Edwin Bennett Pottery (continued)

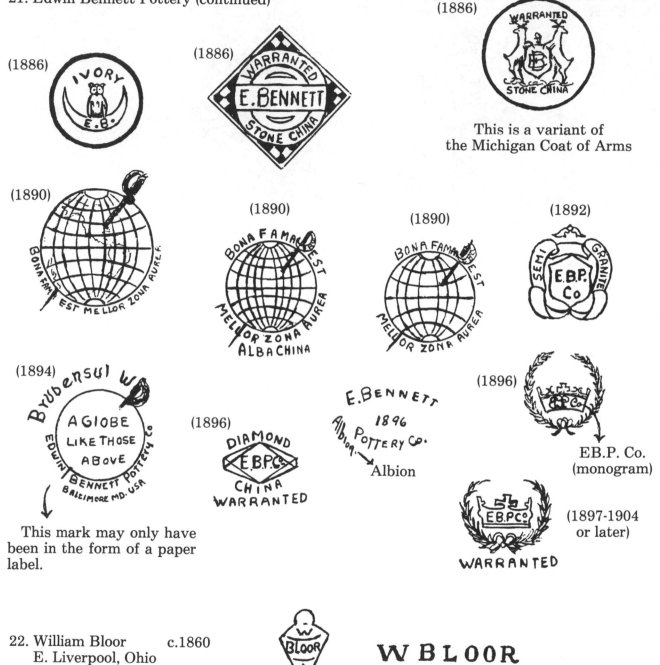

(1886)

(1886)

(1886)

This is a variant of
the Michigan Coat of Arms

(1890)

(1890)

(1890)

(1892)

(1894)

(1896)

(1896)

E. Bennett
1896
Albion. Pottery Co.
→ Albion

EB.P. Co.
(monogram)

(1897-1904
or later)

This mark may only have
been in the form of a paper
label.

22. William Bloor   c.1860
    E. Liverpool, Ohio

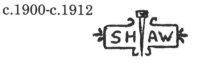

W B L O O R

23. Bonnin and Morris   c.1770   in Philadelphia, Pa.
                marked with a P in blue under the glaze — very rare

24. Bradshaw China Co.   c.1900-c.1912
    Niles, Ohio

25. Brighton Pottery   c.1905
    Zanesville, Ohio
                Their mark is the company name and city in a circle.

16

26. Brockman Pottery Co.   1862-1912
    Cincinnati, Ohio

                  Tempest, Brockmann & Co.   (1862-1881)
                  Tempest, Brockmann & Sampson Pottery Co.   (1881-1887)
                  Brockmann Pottery Co. founded by C.E. Brockmann   (1887-1912)

(before 1881)   (1887-c.1904 or later)

The mark at left may say WARRANTED BEST IRONSTONE CHINA above the mark.

27. William Brunt, Son & Co.   1878-c.1894
    East Liverpool, Ohio

           This company was called William Brunt, Jr. & Co. between 1877 and 1878. Marks included the initials W.B.Jr. & Co.

28. William Brunt Pottery Co.   1894 (or 1892)-1911
    East Liverpool, Ohio

           Barber said this company was incorporated in 1894, as two of the marks below seem to indicate; however, Gates and Ormerod say 1892. See p. 104 of the Appendix for a mark that may have been used by the Brunt Pottery Co. between 1892 and 1894.

(c.1892 and later)

(1894 and later)

(1894 and later)

28. William Brunt Pottery Co. (continued)

(c.1905-c.1911)

NEW ERA
W.B.P. CO.

(c.1905-c.1911)   (mark often in gold)

BRUNT
ART WARE

The following Barber (pre-1904) marks may date back as far as the 1880s when the Brunt Pottery Co. was called William Brunt, Son & Co. They date from c.1880 to c.1904.

ELECTRIC   CHICAGO

Alliance   ROCKET   Chester

29. Brush-McCoy Pottery   1911-1925
Roseville and Zanesville, Ohio
          They made mostly artware; the mark often includes the word MITUSA.

30. Buffalo Pottery Co.   1903 to the present
Buffalo, N.Y.

Early Buffalo Pottery is usually marked with a buffalo, BUF-FALO POTTERY and the date. A later mark, from about World War I onward, is BUFFALO CHINA.
See *The Book of Buffalo Pottery* by Seymour and Violet Altman for more about this company.

31. Burford Bros. Pottery Co.   1879-1904
East Liverpool, Ohio

(1880s)

(c.1880-c.1900)

(c.1880-c.1900)

(c.1880-c.1900)

ELECTRIC

HOTEL

(1890s)

(1890s)
Burford Bros
CHAMPION

(1890s)
BURFORD BROS
BEAUTY

31. Burford Bros. Pottery Co. (continued)

(c.1900-1904)   (c.1900-1904)   (c.1900-1904)

PORCELAIN

PORCELAIN

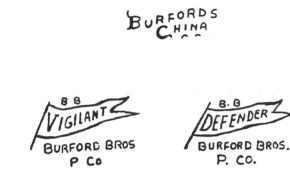

32. Burley & Winter Pottery Co.   1870s-c.1930
    Crooksville, Ohio

They made mostly stoneware. Their mark included the words
BURLEY & WINTER.

33. Burroughs & Mountford Co.   1879-c.1900.
    Trenton, N.J.

B – M

HONITON
B & M Co.

B & M Co.

(c.1892)

B.–M.

B & M
CHINA

34. Cambridge Art Pottery   1895-1909
    Guernsey Earthenware Co.   1909-early 1920s
    Cambridge, Ohio

These first four marks were used before 1909.

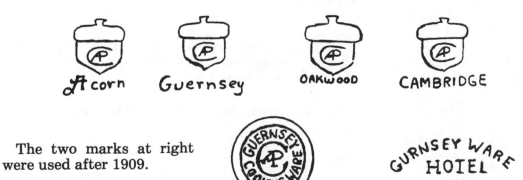

Acorn   Guernsey   OAKWOOD   CAMBRIDGE

The two marks at right
were used after 1909.

19

35. Canonsburg China Co.   1901-c.1909
    Canonsburg, Pa.

36. Canonsburg Pottery Co.   c.1909-1970s
    Canonsburg, Pa.

This company was a reorganized form of the Canonsburg China Co.

37. Carr China Co.   1916-c.1950
    Grafton, W.Va.

CARR CHINA was included as part of this company's mark.

38. Carrollton Pottery Co.   1903-1929
    Carrollton, Ohio

(c.1910-c.1920)

(c.1903-c.1910)

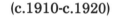

I found the mark at left on a fine American flow blue tureen.

(1920s)

The mark at left was found on a beautiful 1920s covered vegetable dish; however, the quality of the whiteware was terrible. It had the feel of a common red earthenware pot. I don't yet know the meaning of the H in the mark.

39. Cartwright Brothers   c.1880-1927
    East Liverpool, Ohio

Gates and Ormerod say they made their first cream-colored ware and ironstone in 1887. The company was incorporated as the Cartwright Bros. Co. in 1896.

The four marks below were used between c.1887 and c.1904.

(c.1887-c.1896)

TEXAS   Avalon

Brooklyn   Elsmere

39. Cartwright Brothers (continued)

(1887-c.1896)

(1896-c.1905)

(c.1910-c.1920)

THE CARTWRIGHT BROS.CO.

The mark below and the FLORENCE mark are from *The East Liverpool, Ohio, Pottery District* by William C. Gates, Jr. and Dana E. Ormerod.*

(1887-1896)

(1920s)

C.B.P.Co.
MADE IN U.S.A.
CHINA

40. Ceramic Art Co.   See Lenox

41. Chelsea China Co.   1888-c.1900
    New Cumberland, W.Va.

42. Chelsea Keramic Art Works   1866-1891
    Chelsea Pottery, U.S.   1891-1896
    Chelsea, Mass.

(over for marks)

* These Gates and Ormerod marks were published in *Historical Archaeology* Volume 16, Numbers 1 & 2, p.31 and 32.

42. Chelsea Keramic Art Works (continued)

impressed mark
(1875-1889)

impressed mark
(1875-1880)

(1891)

(1893+)

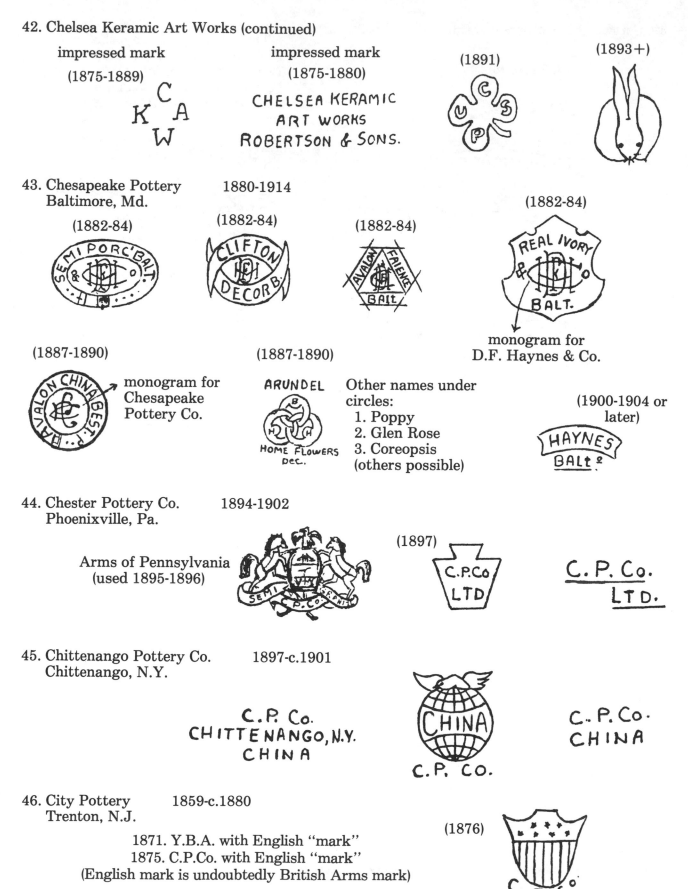

CHELSEA KERAMIC
ART WORKS
ROBERTSON & SONS.

43. Chesapeake Pottery
Baltimore, Md.

1880-1914

(1882-84)

(1882-84)

(1882-84)

(1882-84)

monogram for
D.F. Haynes & Co.

(1887-1890)

monogram for
Chesapeake
Pottery Co.

(1887-1890)

ARUNDEL

HOME FLOWERS DEC.

Other names under
circles:
1. Poppy
2. Glen Rose
3. Coreopsis
(others possible)

(1900-1904 or
later)

HAYNES
BALTº

44. Chester Pottery Co.
Phoenixville, Pa.

1894-1902

Arms of Pennsylvania
(used 1895-1896)

(1897)

C.P.Co
LTD

C. P. Co.
LTD.

45. Chittenango Pottery Co.
Chittenango, N.Y.

1897-c.1901

C. P. Co.
CHITTENANGO, N.Y.
CHINA

CHINA

C. P. CO.

C. P. Co.
CHINA

46. City Pottery
Trenton, N.J.

1859-c.1880

1871. Y.B.A. with English "mark"
1875. C.P.Co. with English "mark"
(English mark is undoubtedly British Arms mark)

(1876)

C. P. Co.

47. Cleveland China Co. or George H. Bowman Co.   1890s-1930s
    Cleveland, Ohio

They distributed and marked pieces made by other companies. Some pieces are of foreign manufacture.

48. Colonial Company   c.1903-c.1930
    E. Liverpool, Ohio

(c.1907)

(1920s)

(c.1910-c.1920)

S - V CHINA
COLONIAL

49. Columbia Art Pottery Co.   1893-c.1902
    Trenton, N.J.

Morris & Willmore founded the company.

COLUMBIAN
TRENTON
N.J.
ART POTTERY

50. Cook Pottery Co.   1894-1920s
    Trenton, N.J.

All but the last mark date from 1904 or earlier.

There is a similar British Arms mark but with a different ribbon above Mellor & Co.

This mark may be found without a co. name or with CH. H.C. under the mark. See page 83.

(1897)

See page 84.

(c.1900-1910)

(after 1904)

51. Coors Porcelain   c.1915-late 1930s
    Golden, Col.

All marks include the word COORS with U.S.A. or Golden, Col. Don't confuse with later H.F. Coors & Co. See pp. 45 & 46 of Lois Lehner's *Complete Book of American Kitchen and Dinner Wares.*

52. Coxon & Co.   1863-1884
    Trenton, N.J.

53. Coxon Pottery   1926-1930
    Wooster, Ohio

They made a fine porcelain called Coxon Belleek.

54. Crescent China Co.   1920s
    Alliance, Ohio

55. Crescent Pottery   1881-c.1906 (perhaps later)
    Trenton, N.J.

This company was founded by Charles Cook & W.S. Hancock.

ARMS OF N.J.   (1890)   (1890)   (1890)

(1885)

(1896)

(1896-98)

(1896-1898)   (1899-1902)   (1900-1902)

This shield may
also have DAINTY
or SEVERN
across it.

This last mark
may have ALPHA
under the circle.

TP. Co. monogram is for
the Trenton Potteries Co.
See page 71.

56. Crooksville China Co.   1902-1959
    Crooksville, Ohio

This is the only mark
given in Barber's 1904
marks book.

(over for more about this co.)

56. Crooksville China Co. (continued)

This company used many marks during its more than 50 years of production; however, most of these marks date from the 1920s and later. Between c.1910 and the early 1920s this company was having problems. The STERLING PORCELAIN mark below is from this early period. At about the same time Crooksville also made whiteware marked STINTHAL CHINA and possibly STERLING CHINA (See p. 92). A mark that includes C.C. Co. as initials or a monogram will be for this company. For more Crooksville marks and information see the Appendix, p. 86.

(c.1910-c.1920)

C.C. Co. monogram

This monogram was in use after 1910; however, its use does not necessarily indicate an early mark.

57. Crown Pottery Co. Evansville, Ind.

1891-c.1960

This first group of marks all date from 1904 and earlier.

An Anchor Pottery mark and a Vodrey Pottery mark are almost identical to this. The main difference is the monogram on the shield. See no. 12 and no. 185.

Crown Porcelain

This mark was used only on dinnerware.

R EX.

CROWN HOTEL WARE

C.P. CO. REX

REGINA
———
C.P. CO

C.P. CO
ROYAL

JEWEL
———
C.P. Co.

ALMA   HELEN.   HOBSON   RENA.

This mark is a virtual copy of Johnson Bros. c.1900 mark. (a British mark)

The next two marks were used before World War I. Crown Pottery Co. worked for jobbers between WWI and the 1930s. Little, if any, of the wares produced during this period was marked. From the 1930s on the mark was CROWN POTTERIES CO.

(c.1905)

SEMI
PORCELAIN
———
C.P. Co.

(c.1910)

58. Croxall Pottery (& Sons) Co.   c.1893-c.1912
    East Liverpool, Ohio

No marks are known for this company.

59. Dedham Pottery   1896-1943
    Dedham, Mass.

This company followed the Chelsea Pottery, U.S. The mark is the famous DEDHAM POTTERY with rabbit.

60. Delaware Pottery   1884-1895
    Trenton, N.J.

They became part of Trenton Potteries in 1895.

61. Denver China & Pottery Co.   1901-1905
    Denver, Col.

62. Derry China Co.   1900-c.1905
    Derry Station, Pa.

63. Dresden Pottery   1876 to at least 1926
    E. Liverpool, Ohio

The marks of this company can be separated into three categories:

I. 1876-c.1882. During this period the company was called Brunt, Bloor, Martin & Co. The mark included B.B.M. & Co.

II. c.1882-c.1915. During this period the various marks usually contain the word DRESDEN.

III. c.1916-c.1926. During this period the mark was POTTERS CO-OPERATIVE CO. or T.P.C-O. Co.

(over for Dresden Pottery marks)

63. Dresden Pottery (Continued)

The Dresden Pottery was organized as the Potters Cooperative Co. in 1882. The cooperative aspects of the company ended soon after. From about 1890 to 1915 the marks of the company nearly always had the word Dresden in the mark.

(c.1890)

The D.P.W. monogram on the mark above is for Dresden Pottery Works.

I found this mark on a teapot with a moss rose decoration. The whiteware was of good quality. Gates and Ormerod show a similar mark with an 1890 date. They also show a number of similar marks with T.P.C. Co. initials (for The Potters Cooperative Co.). These marks also have a P.C. (for Potters Cooperative) monogram in the center of the shield. Don't confuse the early T.P.C. Co. initials with the later (after 1915) T.P.C-O. Co. initials.

(c.1890)

(c.1890)

DRESDEN
WARRANTED
CHINA

(c.1895-c.1900)

DRESDEN
VITREOUS PORCELAIN
EAST LIVERPOOL

(c.1895)

DRESDEN
HOTEL CHINA

(c.1900-c.1910)

DRESDEN
HOTEL CHINA
WARRANTED

The mark above may be impressed or printed.

(c.1895-c.1905)

(c.1900)

(c.1895-c.1900)

The ribbon mark at left may say instead of DRESDEN:
1. CALIFORNIA
2. MADRID
3. PORTLAND
4. YALE

(over for more marks)

63. Dresden Pottery (continued)

(c.1905-1910)   (c.1910-c.1915)

This mark was found on 1910 and 1912 calendar plates.

The marks below were used from about 1915 to 1926. Other marks incorporate these words and initials.

THE POTTERS CO-OPERATIVE CO.   POTTERS CO-OPERATIVE CO.

T. P. C-O. CO.   (See p. 103 for a T.P.C. Co. mark.)

The two marks below are from *The East Liverpool, Ohio, Pottery District* by William C. Gates, Jr. and Dana E. Ormerod. These marks date from 1925 to 1927. These marks were published in *Historical Archaeology* Volume 16, Numbers 1 & 2, p.219.

Dresden
S. V. CHINA
MADE IN U.S.A.
3 26

64. East End Pottery Co.   1894-1909
    East Liverpool, Ohio

For a short time c.1909 this company was called the East End China Co. See the Trenle Co. on p. 70.

(c.1895)   (c.1900)   (c.1904-c.1909)

This mark was found on a 1910 calendar plate. See Trenle China Co., p. 70.

See p. 101 for a similar mark.

The three marks below are pre-1904 marks.

Alaska   DEWEY
           EEP.CO.   *Columbus*

65. East Liverpool Pottery Co.   1894-1900
    East Liverpool, Ohio

(c.1896)   E.L.P. Co.
                                  monogram

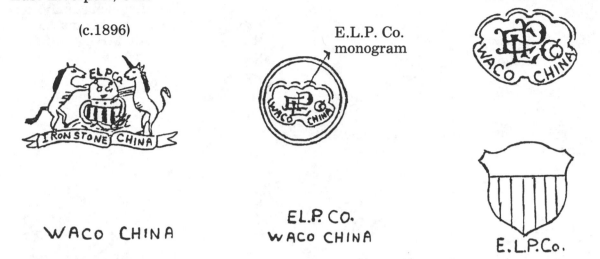

WACO CHINA   EL.P.CO.
                      WACO CHINA   E. L.P.Co.

Some WACO marked whiteware is of excellent quality. It is highly vitrified with no trace of crazing. Two examples looked and felt so much like porcelain I held them to the light to check for translucency. The transfer designs were made by the old copper engraving process; however, they had a delicacy and sophistication not often found in early American whiteware.

66. East Liverpool Potteries Co.   1900-1903 and/or 1907 (See below for an explanation.)
    East Liverpool, Ohio

The East Liverpool Potteries Co. was formed in 1900 from a combination of six smaller companies. This combination failed and in 1903 all member companies left the East Liverpool Potteries except the Globe Pottery and United States Pottery Co. These two companies separated in 1907 and the East Liverpool Potteries Co. ended; however, the United States Pottery Co. of Wellsville, Ohio, continued to use East Liverpool Potteries Co. marks until the 1920s. See the United States Pottery Co. for these later marks.

67. East Morrisania China Works   c.1890-c.1904 (possibly later)
    New York, N.Y.

D. Robitzek was the owner
of the company.

68. East Palestine Pottery Co.   1884-1909
    East Palestine, Ohio

E.P.P. Co. ← monogram

The following may also
be found on this mark:
1. COLUMBIA
2. LAFAYETTE
   PORCELAIN
3. IRIS, etc.

REVERE

69. East Trenton Pottery Co.   c.1885-c.1905
    Trenton, N.J.

(1888)

IRONSTONE CHINA
E.T. P CO.

IRONSTONE CHINA
E.T P Co.

E.T.P.CO.

OPAQUE CHINA
E.T. P. Co.

impressed mark

70. Empire Pottery of Alpaugh & Magowan   1884-1892 (perhaps to WWI)
    Trenton, N.J.

(1884)

IRONSTONE CHINA
A & M

(c.1888)

IMPERIAL
WARRANTED
CHINA
(often impressed)

(1892)

EMPIRE

TRENTON
N.J.

A wreath mark with EMPIRE CHINA in gold (circa 1910)
may be for this company; however, I believe it is for an East
Liverpool, Ohio company. See p. 83.

71. Enterprise Pottery Co.   c.1880-1892
    Trenton, N.J.

Enterprise
Pottery Co

72. Faience Manufacturing Co.   1880-1892
    Greenpoint, N.Y.

(over for marks)

72. Faience Manufacturing Co. (continued)

(c.1880)   (c.1885)   (1886-1892)

incised mark

73. Fell & Thropp Co.   c.1880-c.1893
    Trenton, N.J.

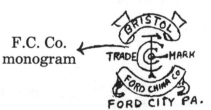

74. Ford China Co.   c.1890-1910
    Ford City, Pa.

F.C. Co.
monogram ←

The upper ribbon may
also say:
1. DERBY
2. LEEDS
3. TURIN
4. VICTOR
5. others also

75. Franklin Pottery Co.   1880-1884
    Franklin, Ohio

$$\frac{F\ P\ C}{F}$$

The dates and the mark
are from John Ramsay.

76. Fraunfelter China Co.   c.1920-1930s
    Zanesville, Ohio

They made a hard-paste porcelain. Their mark includes the
word FRAUNFELTER.

77. French China Co.   c.1900-1934.
    Sebring, Ohio

From 1916 to 1934 the company was owned by the Sebring
Manufacturing Co.; however, the French China name continued
to be used. In 1934 the French Saxon China Co. was formed.

(over for marks)

77. French China Co. (continued)

These first seven marks are from Barber's 1904 marks book.

La Française Porcelain

Greek

Kenneth

These French China Co. marks date from 1905 to c.1930.

(c.1905-c.1915)   (c.1919)   (1920s)

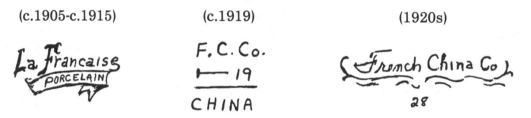

This French China Co. mark has two forms. The earlier mark looks more like a three-plumes (Prince of Wales' Crest) mark; the later mark is a fleur-de-lis. It is more stylized than the earlier mark. The earlier mark was in use as early as 1907 (on 1907 calendar plate), perhaps as early as 1904. See below. The A 4 might indicate 1904.

(c.1905-c.1915)   (used after WWI)

The A 4 was not on the 1907 calendar plate.

78. Fulper Pottery   1860-1930s
    Flemington, N.Y.

They made mostly art pottery.

See *Art Pottery of the United States* by Paul Evans.

79. Geijsbeek Pottery Co.   1899-1904 (or later)
    Denver & Golden, Col.

(over for marks)

79. Geijsbeek Pottery Co. (continued)

(1899-1900)

GEIJSBEEK POTTERY CO.
DENVER, COLO.

(1899-1900)

G. P. C.

(1900)

This 1900 mark may have word GOLDEN in the center.

(1901 onward)

80. W.S. George Pottery
Canonsburg, Pa.

c.1909-1955

Mr. George had an interest in a number of factories, and the W.S. George mark was used at several of them. Most wares with his mark will not be early. The mark below may have been used at any of the George factories.

(c.1920)

81. W.S. George Pottery
East Palestine, Ohio

1909-late 1950s

(c.1910) W. S. GEORGE
POTTERY CO.
EAST PALESTINE, O.

See No. 80 for more on W.S. George.

82. Glasgow Pottery
Trenton, N.J.

1863-1905

(c.1870)

GLASGOW POTTERY
-CO.-
TRENTON
N. J.

(1876)

IRONSTONE CHINA
J. M. & Co.

This eagle mark, without ironstone china, used on semi-porcelain in 1878.

(1880)

JOHN MOSES

(1884)

(1882)

(1893)

(c.1890)

(over for more marks)

33

82. Glasgow Pottery (continued)

These two marks were used before 1895.

(c.1890)

(c.1890)

Note the G.P. Co. monogram on the shield to the left.

The following marks all date from 1895 to 1905. The use of J.M.&S. on the mark confirms that it was not used before 1895.

83. Globe Pottery Co.   1888-1900; 1907-1912
     East Liverpool, Ohio

This company was part of the East Liverpool Potteries Co. from 1901 to 1907.

(1896)

The mark at left may have the words FESTOON or PROGRESS accompanying the mark.

(1896)

(1897)

Made by
GlobePottery Co.
E. L.,O.

83. Globe Pottery Co. (continued)

(1898)

(c.1900)

(1907-1912)

The above mark may have a globe with wings.

(c.1900)

HOTEL
G P CO

84. Goodwin Brothers   1876-1893
    Goodwin Pottery Co.   1893-1912

(c.1880)

(c.1885)

(c.1890)

(after 1893)

GOODWIN'S
HOTEL CHINA

(1893-c.1904)

(after 1893)

See p. 87 of the Appendix for more about the Goodwin Pottery Co.

85. Greenwood Pottery
    Trenton, N.J.

1868-c.1900

    This company may have succumbed to the Panic of 1893. All the Barber marks date before 1893. In his 1904 book he used the past tense when mentioning this company. The only later mark I have seen has GREENWOOD CHINA, 1862-1876. This mark looks like a 1930s mark. There is probably no connection with it and the old Greenwood Pottery.

(over for marks)

85. Greenwood Pottery (continued)

(1868-1875)   (1868-1875)   (1883-1886)   (1886)

G.P.
Co.

(1886)

GREENWOOD CHINA
TRENTON, N.J.

impressed mark

(1886)

86. Grueby Faience (Pottery) Co.   1897-1911
    Boston, Mass.

They made art pottery. Their mark includes the word
GRUEBY.

87. Haeger Potteries Inc.   1914-present
    Dundee, Ill.

They made some early art pottery; they made no early
whiteware.

88. Hall China Co.   1903-present
    E. Liverpool, Ohio

Collectors are primarily interested in later products of this
company. Products of the 1930s and 1940s are of interest. Hall's
Autumn Leaf is widely collected. There is not a great amount of
Hall whiteware that dates before 1920. The early marks mostly
have HALL CHINA CO. E.L.O. (1903-c.1914).

(c.1905)

 (used early; but also
used late)

 (used mostly in 1920s)

89. Hampshire Pottery   1871-1923
    Keene, N.H.

These two marks were used mostly on whiteware souvenir pieces for
sale at summer resorts of the early 1900s.

These marks are printed in red. The signature in center is J.S. Taft. They date from c.1900 to c.1916.

(over for more marks)

36

89. Hampshire Pottery (continued)

In addition to the souvenir ware, they made ordinary whiteware as well as considerable art pottery. See Paul Evans' *Art Pottery of the United States*. Ordinary whiteware may not have been marked; some art pottery was marked as given below.

Hampshire Pottery

J S T & CO
KEENE, N.H

90. Harker Pottery Co.   1840s-c.1970   (c.1892)
East Liverpool, Ohio

 This mark was impressed on yellowware and Rockingham from 1847 to 1850.

(1890-c.1910)

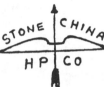

Barber said that the mark above was used on a portrait plate decorated by Harker for the Burroughs & Mountford Co. whose impressed mark was also on the plate.

Barber gave the 1892 date. The mark may be one used by Harker to indicate decorating for other companies.

(1879-1890)    (1890-1920s)

91. Herold Pottery   1910-1915
Golden, Col.

It became Coors Porcelain. See p. 98 for possible mark.

92. Hull Pottery   1905-present
Crooksville, Ohio

They are best known for their art pottery made after WWI; their earlier products were mostly kitchenware-type items.

These impressed marks were used from c.1908 to c.1930.

93. Huntington China Co.   1904-1911
Huntington, W.Va.

No marks are known.

94. Illinois China Co.   c.1920-1946
Lincoln, Ill.

Their mark was ILLINOIS CHINA CO. around a circle with a large I in the center.

95. International Pottery Co.   1860-1920s
    Trenton, N.J.

These marks date from 1879 to c.1903. Marks after 1903 include Burgess & Co., I.P.CO. and possibly International Pottery Co. See p. 83 for a later mark of this company.

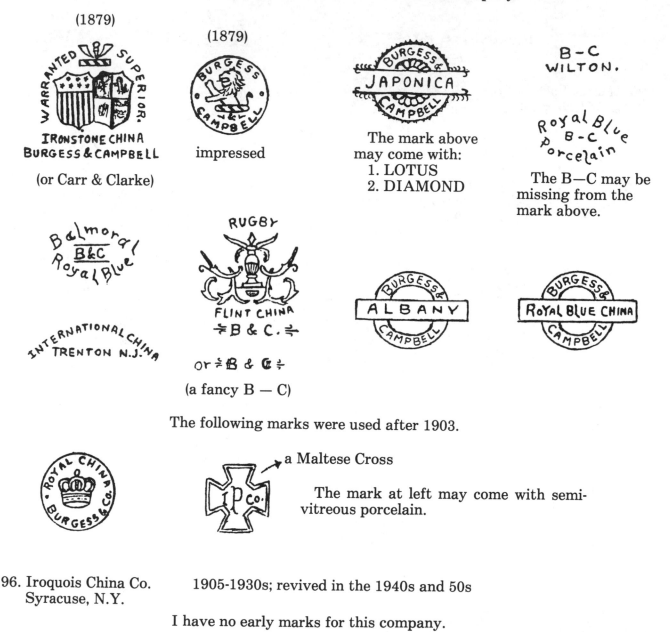

(1879)

IRONSTONE CHINA
BURGESS & CAMPBELL

(or Carr & Clarke)

(1879)

impressed

The mark above
may come with:
1. LOTUS
2. DIAMOND

B-C
WILTON.

Royal Blue
B-C
Porcelain

The B—C may be
missing from the
mark above.

Balmoral
B&C
Royal Blue

INTERNATIONAL CHINA
TRENTON N.J.

RUGBY

FLINT CHINA
B & C.

or B & C.

(a fancy B — C)

ALBANY

ROYAL BLUE CHINA

The following marks were used after 1903.

a Maltese Cross

The mark at left may come with semi-vitreous porcelain.

96. Iroquois China Co.   1905-1930s; revived in the 1940s and 50s
    Syracuse, N.Y.

I have no early marks for this company.

97. Jersey City Pottery   1820s-1892.
    Jersey City, N.J.

The earliest marks all had Jersey City and/or American Pottery (Co.) on them. They would be quite rare. About 1850 they became the first American potters to make whiteware exclusively. They began to make whiteware in 1840 and were the first to make it a commercial success.

(over for marks)

97. Jersey City Pottery (continued)

(1850s)

R & T
(Rouse & Turner)

(1880s)   ⟨ɪ.v.w.⟩

98. Keswick China Co.   c.1900+
    Fallston, Pa.

 No marks are known for this company.

99. Keystone Pottery Company   1890 to c.1910
    Rochester & New Brighton, Pa.

 No marks are known. This mark below is from a c.1950 company.

(c.1950)   KEYSTONE

CHINA

100. Keystone Pottery Co.   1892-1930s
     Trenton, N.J.

 They made mostly sanitary ware. This is a Barber (pre-1904) mark.

101. Edwin M. Knowles China Co.   1901-1963*
     East Liverpool, Ohio

 Interestingly, there were only two marks used by this company during its first 25 years. The company initials were used only for a few years.

(c.1904)   E.M.K
           C. CO.

 The Knowles vase (looks like balloon) mark was used from 1901 to 1948. For most of the time, from c.1901 to c.1925, it was the only mark of the company. However, it is possible to date the mark by using several means. The most important is the Knowles dating system. From 1901 to 1909 the vase mark will have no numbers or two numbers (possibly a number and a letter) under the mark. From 1910 to c.1914 there are three digits under the mark. From 1915 to c.1930 there are three separate numbers under the mark. The first indicates the year.

* The Edwin M. Knowles name is again in use on limited edition ware.

101. Edwin M. Knowles China Co. (continued)

112	1911
15 1 11	1915
16-2-4	1916
23-3 6	1923
24-1-11	1924
30 2-3	1930

The vase may say VITREOUS or SEMI VITREOUS.

EDWIN M. KNOWLES CHINA CO. 15 1 11

During the 1930s the vase mark was seldom (perhaps never) used. The mark used then was the ship mark given below. There are two numbers under the mark. The first indicates the year; the second indicates the month. The ship mark is said to have been used before the 1930s; so far, I have not seen one.

32-2	1932 (Feb.)
34-12	1934 (Dec.)
35-3	1935 (Mar.)
38-10	1938 (Oct.)

MADE IN U.S.A. was used after 1930.

During the 1940s the vase mark was again in use; however, it is a bit different from the earlier mark. The crosshatching is wider on the later mark. See comparison below:

EARLY MARK

(bottom of vase)

6 central diamonds

LATER MARK

(bottom of vase)

5 central diamonds

The dating for the 1940s is the same as the 1930s.

43-1	1943 (Jan.)
45-8	1945 (Aug.)
48 8	1948 (Aug.)

MADE IN U.S.A. was used after 1930.

EDWIN M. KNOWLES CHINA CO. MADE IN U.S.A.

On some 1948 marks the word KNOWLES is printed across the vase.

102. Knowles, Taylor and Knowles Co.   1854-1929
     East Liverpool, Ohio

   This company is the epitome of the early American whiteware industry. Its history covers nearly the entire period this book attempts to cover. Companies like Knowles, Taylor and Knowles helped to make East Liverpool, Ohio, the center of the American whiteware industry.

   Their first whiteware dates back to 1872.

   This earliest mark is from *The East Liverpool, Ohio Pottery District* by William C. Gates, Jr. and Dana E. Ormerod.*

(1872-c.1878)

Buffalo marks:
                    These marks were used between 1878 and 1885.

      There are a number of variations of the buffalo mark.

Eagle trademark of the company:
                    These marks date from c.1880 to c.1890.

* This Gates and Ormerod mark was published in *Historical Archaeology*, Volume 16, Numbers 1 & 2, p.116.

Eagle trademark of the company (continued):

These marks and variations of these marks were used from c.1880 to c.1905. This mark with BELLEEK dates to c.1890.

(c.1880)

Eagle under monogram mark:

These marks and variations of them date from c.1890 to c.1918. Above the mark is a K.T.K. (second K is backward) monogram.

(c.1890-1907)

State, City or College marks:

These marks indicate shapes, decorations or patterns. They date from c.1885 to c.1905. All of these were listed in Barber's 1904 book. For much more about these and other K.T.&K. marks see *The East Liverpool, Ohio, Pottery District* by William C. Gates and Dana E. Ormerod.*

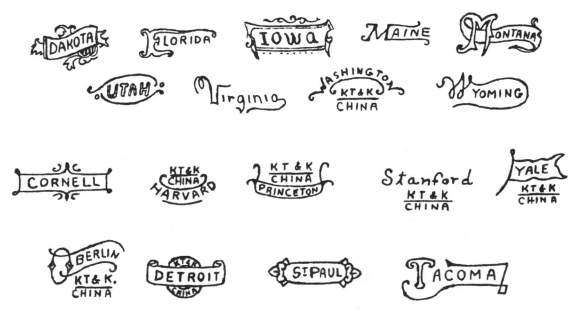

* This work was published in *Historical Archaeology* Volume 16, Numbers 1 & 2, (1982).

102. Knowles, Taylor and Knowles Co. (continued)

Other State marks; other shape marks:

The mark to the left was used from c.1905 to c.WWI. Gates and Ormerod showed a CALIFORNIA mark dating it c.1890. They listed the following shape marks used from 1905: FANCY, QUINCY, ROCHESTER and LUNA.

Other Knowles, Taylor and Knowles marks:

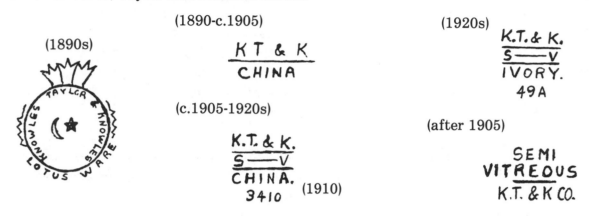

(1890s)

(1890-c.1905)

K T & K
CHINA

(c.1905-1920s)

K.T. & K.
S——V
CHINA.
3410   (1910)

(1920s)

K.T. & K.
S——V
IVORY.
49A

(after 1905)

SEMI
VITREOUS
K.T. & K CO.

Knowles, Taylor and Knowles did use a dating system. The system may have had limited use; however, some marks used between 1905 (perhaps earlier) and WWI used the following system: Three digits were used from 1905 to 1909; the last digit indicates the year. From 1910 on four digits were used; the last two digits indicate the year.

315	(1905)	3410	(1910)
236	(1906)	3012	(1912)

103. Kurlbaum & Swartz   1851-1855
     Philadelphia, Pa.

They made early hard-paste porcelain.

K & S (very rare mark)

104. Homer Laughlin China Co.   1877 to the present
     East Liverpool, Ohio

As Knowles, Taylor & Knowles epitomizes the early American whiteware industry, Homer Laughlin epitomizes the industry as it moved into the modern period. This company's development of continuous tunnel kiln in 1923 could well be considered the watershed of the American early and modern periods.

Laughlin's early practice of dating individual wares and his early trademark with the American Eagle atop a vanquished British Lion are also noteworthy.

See the next two pages as well as pp. 88 and 89 for marks and information about Homer Laughlin.

104. Homer Laughlin China Co. (continued)

Homer Laughlin's Dating System (1900 onward) is as follows:

1900-1920   There are three numbers on the mark: the first number (1-12) is for the month of the year; the second number (0-20) represents the year; the final number (from 1910 it's a letter) indicates the factory where the item was made.

1900	(1-12)	0	(factory no. (1, 2, 3)	1910	(1-12)	10	(factory letter)	
1901	(1-12)	1	" "	1911	(1-12)	11	" "	
1902	(1-12)	2	" "	1912	(1-12)	12	" "	
1903	(1-12)	3	" "	1913	(1-12)	13	" "	
1904	(1-12)	4	" "	1914	(1-12)	14	" "	
1905	(1-12)	5	" "	1915	(1-12)	15	" "	
1906	(1-12)	6	" "	1916	(1-12)	16	" "	
1907	(1-12)	7	" "	1917	(1-12)	17	" "	
1908	(1-12)	8	" "	1918	(1-12)	18	" "	
1909	(1-12)	9	" "	1919	(1-12)	19	" "	
				1920	(1-12)	20	" "	

There may be some deviation from the above system. A single digit may be used for the years 1911 to 1919, particularly if the month number has two digits. For example: 11 9 L might be used for Nov. 1919. The L indicates the factory.

1921-1929   A letter (not a number) now indicates the month of the year (A-L); a single digit number indicates the year (1-9); a final letter (or letter and number) still indicates the factory. N5 is common as a factory indicator.

1921	(A-L)	1	(factory letter)	1925	(A-L)	5	(factory letter)
also:	(no.)	21	(factory letter)	1926	(A-L)	6	" "
	used in 1921.			1927	(A-L)	7	" "
1922	(A-L)	2	(factory letter)	1928	(A-L)	8	" "
1923	(A-L)	3	(factory letter)	1929	(A-L)	9	" "
1924	(A-L)	4	(factory letter)				

Made In U.S.A. first appeared on 1922 or 1923 marks.

From 1930 on, the middle number is the year itself; for example: 32 is used for 1932, 45 is for 1945, etc.

Before 1877 a mark with LAUGHLIN BROS. under a shield was used.

(1877-c.1890)

PREMIUM STONE CHINA
HOMER LAUGHLIN

(c.1890-c.1900)

104. Homer Laughlin China Co. (continued)

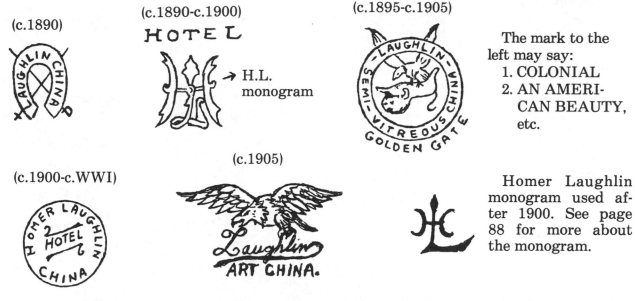

(c.1890)

(c.1890-c.1900)

HOTEL → H.L. monogram

(c.1895-c.1905)

The mark to the left may say:
1. COLONIAL
2. AN AMERI-CAN BEAUTY, etc.

(c.1900-c.WWI)

(c.1905)

Laughlin ART CHINA.

Homer Laughlin monogram used after 1900. See page 88 for more about the monogram.

Most products made by Homer Laughlin after 1900 are marked with an H L C monogram and/or Homer Laughlin. For many more later marks of this company see *The East Liverpool, Ohio, Pottery District* by William C. Gates, Jr. and Dana E. Ormerod.*

105. Lenox, Inc. (Ceramic Art Co.)   1889 to the present
Trenton, N.J.

CERAMIC ART CO. in a wreath used on special decorative work in the late 1800s.

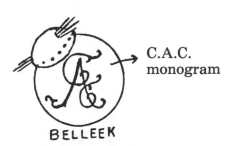

→ C.A.C. monogram

BELLEEK

The mark above was used on both decorated and undecorated (mostly for "home" decorating) wares between 1889 and 1896. Undecorated ware continued to have this mark until 1906.

INDIAN CHINA

LENOX

(before 1895)

(1896-1906)
decorated ware

After 1924 the L in a wreath was used on all wares. MADE IN U.S.A. was first used in 1930.

LENOX

(1906-1924)
decorated ware

BELLEEK

(1906-1924)
undecorated ware

* This work was published in *Historical Archaeology* Volume 16, Numbers 1 & 2, (1982).

106. Lewis Pottery Co.   1830s
     Louisville, Ky.

       They made cream-colored ware for a few years; no marks are known.

107. Limoges China Co.   1900-c.1955
     Sebring, Ohio

       For a short time this company was called the Sterling China Co. For more about Sterling China marks see p. 92.

(c.1900-c.1910)   (c.1905-c.1915)   (c.1915-c.1925)

   LIMOGES   (1920s)
                            CHINA

108. Maddock companies   1882-c.1929
     Trenton, N.J.

       Thomas Maddock & Sons   1882-c.1902

       dinnerware      sanitary
                                                     ware

       Thomas Maddock's Sons Co.   1902-c.1929

(c.1902)      (c.1905-c.1915)

                                            Thos. Maddock's
                                            Son's Co.
                                            Trenton, N.J.

       Maddock Pottery Co.   1893-c.1920

(c.1900)   (c.1900)   (c.1900-c.1912)   M
                                                                       CHINA
   L

                                                (c.1910-c.1920)

                                                                       M
                                                                       LAMBERTON
                                                                       CHINA

108. Maddock companies (continued)

John Maddock (son of Thomas) & Sons   1894-1920s

Barber said this mark was used on "Coalport" china. They made mostly sanitary and specialty wares.

(c.1904)

VITREOUS GLAZE may be above the mark at left.

109. Maryland Pottery Co.   1879-c.1910
Baltimore, Md.

The D.F. Haynes connected with this company for about two years, later acquired the Chesapeake Pottery in 1882. After 1891 this company was making vitreous sanitary ware exclusively.

(1879-1881)

(1879-1881)

(1880-1892)

(1881-1883)

(1883-1891)

ARMS OF MARYLAND

(1881-1885)

C R E M O R N E
OPAQUE
PORCELAIN.

(1887-1890)

STONE CHINA
WARRANTED

(1885-1887)

ETRUSCAN

(not majolica)

110. Mayer Pottery Co.   1881-WWI
Beaver Falls, Pa.

About 1916 this company began to make hotel china. The mark became MAYER CHINA.

Though many, the early Mayer marks are easy to identify. With one exception, J. & E. Mayer is on the mark. The mark that does not, has the initials J. & E. M.

(over for marks)

110. Mayer Pottery Co. (continued)

(1881-1891)   (1890s)   (1890s)   (1890s)

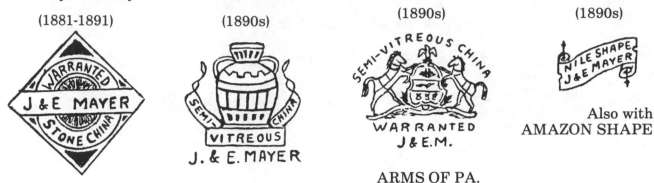

ARMS OF PA.   Also with AMAZON SHAPE

Barber said there were three other special marks used before 1896. They were *Diana, Potomac* and *Windsor.* He did not picture them, however. The following date from about 1900. Some may date to after 1904.

in addition to LINCOLN, the mark at left comes with:
1. GENOA
2. JUNO
3. DAYBREAK
4. DUQUESNE

This mark dates from c.1905 to c.1915.

MARINE

J. & E. MAYER.

111. J.W. McCoy Pottery   1900-1911
Roseville, Ohio

      They had no marks except on a few art pottery items. See Paul Evans' *Art Pottery of the United States.*

112. Nelson McCoy   1910 to the present
Roseville, Ohio

      They made no early whiteware.

113. McNicol potteries (various)
McNicol, Burton & Co.   c.1870-1892
East Liverpool, Ohio

(c.1880-1892)

McN. B. & Co. used on various marks.

D.E. McNicol Pottery   1892-1950s
East Liverpool, Ohio

      As did many others, D.E. McNicol had troubles in the 1920s. They left East Liverpool for a plant they had in West Virginia. Here they survived the Depression making McNICOL CHINA.

(c.1892-c.1900)   (c.1905)

The mark to the left is from *The East Liverpool, Ohio, Pottery District* by William C. Gates and Dana E. Ormerod. A similar mark without company name is on p. 104.*

      The following D.E. McNicol marks are most likely to be encountered by the collector. Since they made much specialty ware, calendar plates, commemorative items and the like, much has survived for us to find today.

(c.1910-c.1915)

(c.1905-c.1920)

(c.1915-c.1923)

CARNATION
McNicol

D.E. McNicol
POTTERY Co.
EAST LIVERPOOL
OHIO

D.E. McNicol
EAST LIVERPOOL,O

* This Gates and Ormerod mark was published in *Historical Archaeology* Volume 16, Numbers 1 & 2, p.186.

D.E. McNicol (continued)

(c.1920)

D.E. McNicol
CLARKSBURG, W.VA.
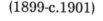

(c.1920)

Marks with McNICOL CHINA or VITRIFIED CHINA date from the 1930s to the 1950s.

See Appendix for more on D.E. McNicol.

T.A. McNicol Pottery Co.   1913-1929
East Liverpool, Ohio

T.A. McNICOL
POTTERY CO.
6 23

T.A. McNicol was a brother of D.E. McNicol. Note how similar this mark is to one of the D.E. McNicol marks. Also, note the dating system. The last two numbers indicate the year: in this case 1923.

McNicol-Smith Company   1899-1907
McNicol-Corns Company   1907-1928
Corns China Company   1928-1932
Wellsville, Ohio

The following marks are from *The East Liverpool, Ohio, Pottery District* by William C. Gates, Jr. and Dana E. Ormerod. I have taken the liberty of correcting the dates for the marks. Gates and Ormerod give both 1889 and 1899 as the year McNicol-Smith was started. Since they were located in the old Baum building, and since Baum was in business until at least 1895 (possibly as late as 1898), this would make the 1889 date impossible.

I doubt that many collectors will come across McNicol-Smith marks. I have never seen one. However, since they were in operation for some time, I felt it was wise to include them. McNicol-Corns marks are likely to be found.

(1907-1928)

(1899-c.1901)   (1899-c.1907)

The center of the c.1903 mark above is an M. & S. monogram.

The four Gates and Ormerod marks shown above were published in *Historical Archaeology* Vol. 16, Numbers 1 & 2, p.196.

114. Mercer Pottery Co.   1868-c.1930
Trenton, N.J.

Mercer Pottery is typical of the Trenton potteries. While many of these companies continued to about the time of the Great Depression, very little of what can be found of their ware dates from beyond the very early 1900s. Most of the Trenton companies that continued into the 20th century converted to making sanitary porcelain (bathtubs, etc.). Therefore, the collector is more likely to find early Trenton whiteware than later ware. Barber's 1904 marks book is still reasonably valid with regard to Trenton potteries.

The following are Barber (pre-1904) marks.

(c.1879)

(c.1880)

(1880s)

impressed mark

(1880s)

MERCER POTTERY
TRENTON N.J.

impressed mark

(c.1890)

These two marks include complex M.P.Co. monograms.

(1890s)

(1890s)

The mark to the left may have SEMI VITREOUS under the mark.

(1890s)

(c.1900)

(c.1900)

(c.1900)

The mark to the left also comes with:
1. TRINIDAD
2. SMYRNA
3. ARDMORE

(c.1900)

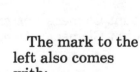

51

115. Millington, Astbury & Poulson   1859-1862
    Trenton, N.J.

116. Morgan Belleek China Co.   1924-1931
    Canton, Ohio

          Wares are marked MORGAN BELLEEK.

117. Morley & Co.   1879-c.1884
    Wellsville, Ohio

George Morley & Son   1885-c.1890
East Liverpool, Ohio

     These marks are from *The East Liverpool, Ohio, Pottery District* by William Gates & Dana Ormerod. They were published in *Historical Archaeology* Vol. 16, Numbers 1 & 2, p.200.

     Another mark had two horses, the U.S. Shield, ironstone china on a ribbon under the shield, and G.M. & Son above the mark.

118. Mount Clemens Pottery   1915-1960s
    Mount Clemens, Mich.

MADE IN U.S.A.
535H   (1935)

119. George C. Murphy & Co.   c.1898-1904
East Liverpool, Ohio

(1898-1901)

(1898-1901)

(1898-1901)

Note the G.C.M.
& Co. monogram
on the mark above.

Paris
J C CM & Co

MURPHY & CO.
VITREOUS
HOTEL PORCELAIN

(1898-1901)

Manhattan

(c.1903)

SEMI
M & Co
PORCELAIN

120. Mutual China Co.   1915-1970s
Indianapolis, Ind.

They were a retailing concern that marked both foreign and American wares.

121. National China Co.   1900-1929
East Liverpool and
Salineville, Ohio

The National China Co. moved to Salineville in 1911. Apparently the company did not prosper well after the move. Most of what I have seen from this company are from the East Liverpool period. I have seen only a few items with Salineville marks. Gates and Ormerod show many marks (actually the stamps for possible marks) from this Salineville period. I have not included these because I doubt that the collector will come across them.

(1900-1911)

N.C.Co.
—————
E.L.O.

(1900-1911)

The NATIONAL
CHINA Co.
—————
E.L.O.

(1900-1911)

NATIONAL
CHINA

(1900-1911)

WESTERN GEM CO. E.L.O.
NATIONAL CHINA CO.

(after 1911)

NATIONAL
CHINA
COMPANY

(c.1918-c.1928)

NATIONAL
CHINA
SALINEVILLE, O.

Variations of the monogram at left were used on several National China Co. marks used after 1911. National Dinner-Ware mark used at this time.

53

122. New Castle Pottery Co.   1901-1905
     New Castle, Pa.

NEW CASTLE CHINA
NEW CASTLE, PA.

123. New England Pottery Co.   1875-c.1914
     East Boston, Mass.

A pottery was established in East Boston as early as 1854 for the manufacture of whiteware. In 1875 Thomas Gray and L.W. Clark took over the pottery, now called the New England Pottery Co.

(1878-1883)   (pre-1904)   (1883-1886)   (1886-1888)

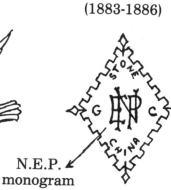

N.E.P.
monogram

RIETI

(1888-1889)

(1887-c.1904)   N.E.P.
                       monogram

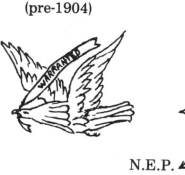

(1897-1904 or later)

N.E.P.
monogram   (1886-1892)

(1889-1895)

(1897-1904 or later)

124. New Jersey Pottery Co.   1869-1883
     Trenton, N.J.

54

125. New Milford Pottery Co.   1886-1903
New Milford, Conn.

This company began making ordinary whiteware. Between 1890 and 1892 the company changed hands and became known as the Wannopee Pottery. Art pottery became important after the change. The names Lang & Schafer and Lang & Osgood were associated with these companies. See Paul Evans' *Art Pottery of the United States.*

New Milford Pottery Co. marks   1886-c.1891

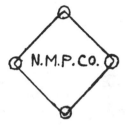

Wannopee Pottery marks   c.1891-1903

126. New Orleans Porcelain Mnfg. Co.   1880s
New Orleans, La.

No marks are known.

127. New York City Pottery   1853-1888
N.Y., N.Y.

Morrison & Carr were the first owners; from 1871 to 1888 James Carr operated the company alone.

(1871)

(1871)

(1860)

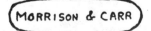

impressed mark

J.C.
monogram

Special mark for
the James L. Howard Co.

127. New York City Pottery (continued)

(1879)   The next five marks date from c.1872 to 1888.

This mark was used on hotel china.

128. Ohio China Co.   c.1890-1912
East Palestine, Ohio

(c.1904)

129. Ohio Pottery Co.   c.1900-1923
Zanesville, Ohio

Charles Fraunfelter took over this company in 1915. Soon after they began to make kitchen and dinner wares. Lois Lehner said they developed a true hard-paste porcelain marked PETROSCAN. From 1923 to the 1930s this company became the Fraunfelter China Co. The name Fraunfelter is on the mark.

130. Ohio Valley China Co.   1887-c.1894
Wheeling, W.Va.

They were first called the West Virginia China Co. Barber said they made a true porcelain of excellent design.

O.V.

131. Oliver China Co. 1899-1909
     Sebring, Ohio

THE OLIVER
CHINA CO
SEBRING OHIO

VERUS
PORCELAIN

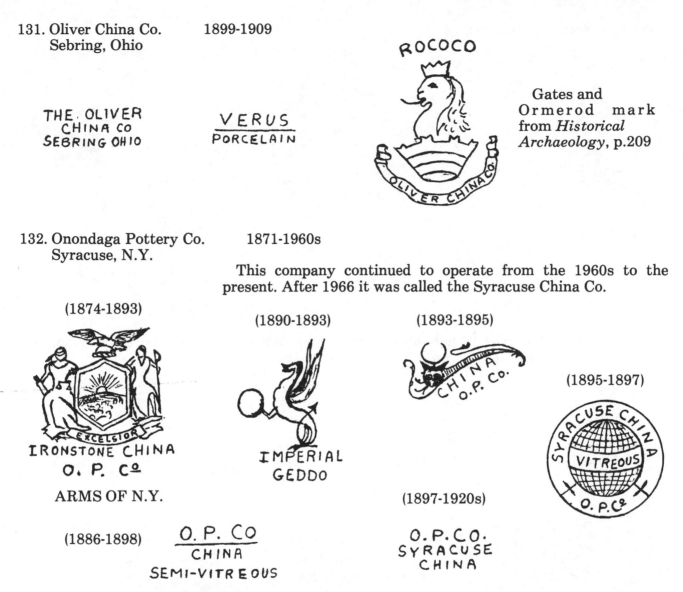

Gates and Ormerod mark from *Historical Archaeology*, p.209

132. Onondaga Pottery Co. 1871-1960s
     Syracuse, N.Y.

This company continued to operate from the 1960s to the present. After 1966 it was called the Syracuse China Co.

(1874-1893)

IRONSTONE CHINA
O. P. Cº
ARMS OF N.Y.

(1890-1893)

IMPERIAL
GEDDO

(1893-1895)

CHINA
O. P. Co.

(1895-1897)

SYRACUSE CHINA
VITREOUS
O. P. Cº

(1886-1898)

O. P. CO
CHINA
SEMI-VITREOUS

(1897-1920s)

O. P. CO.
SYRACUSE
CHINA

Onondaga had a dating system; however, I am not sure how commonly it was used. A number in a circle denotes the years 1903 to 1911. A number in a diamond denotes 1912 to 1919. The letter A with the mark indicates 1920; B is for 1921, etc.

133. Ott & Brewer 1863-1893
     Trenton, N.J.

The Etruria Pottery started in 1863; it became known as Ott & Brewer after 1865. These first two marks were used in the 1870s.

O.&B.
monogram

IRONSTONE CHINA

O.&B.
monogram

STONE CHINA

133. Ott & Brewer (continued)

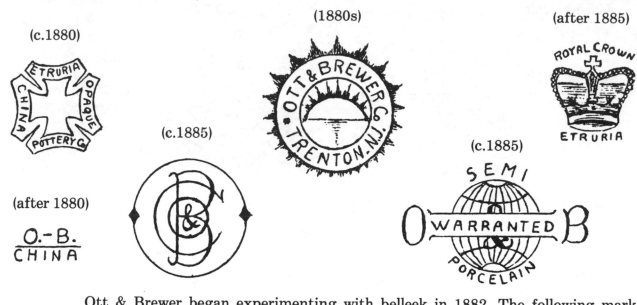

(c.1880)

(1880s)

(after 1885)

(c.1885)

(after 1880)

O.-B.
CHINA

(c.1885)

Ott & Brewer began experimenting with belleek in 1882. The following marks were all belleek marks dating after 1882 to 1893.

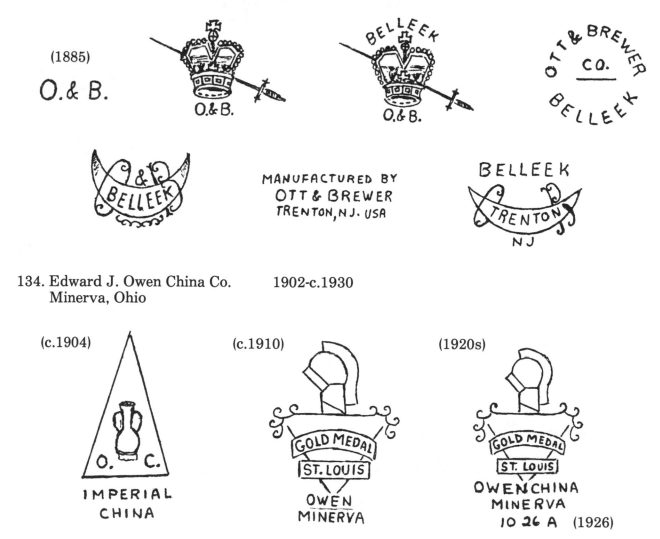

(1885)

O.& B.

134. Edward J. Owen China Co.   1902-c.1930
     Minerva, Ohio

(c.1904)

IMPERIAL
CHINA

(c.1910)

GOLD MEDAL
ST. LOUIS
OWEN
MINERVA

(1920s)

GOLD MEDAL
ST. LOUIS
OWEN CHINA
MINERVA
10 26 A   (1926)

58

135. J.B. Owens Pottery   1885-1907
     Zanesville, Ohio

They made mostly art pottery. See Paul Evans' *Art Pottery of the United States*.

136. Oxford Pottery   1914-1925
     Cambridge, Ohio

They made mostly utilitarian kitchen ware; I am not sure if it was marked. Note: items marked OXFORD WARE or OXFORD STONEWARE were made by Universal Potteries in the 1930s or later.

137. Paden City Pottery Co.   c.1910-1963
     Paden City, W.Va.

They made their first whiteware in the 1920s; most Paden City ware dates from the 1930s and later.

138. Peoria Pottery Co.   1873-1904
     Peoria, Ill.

The American Pottery Co. made whiteware in Peoria from 1859 to c.1863. The company was taken over by others who did not make whiteware again until the 1880s.

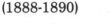

This impressed mark was used between 1860 and c.1863.

(1888-1890)

The above mark may have the words WARRANTED BEST IRONSTONE CHINA printed above the mark.

(1890-1899)

P.P.Co. monogram

(1890-1904)

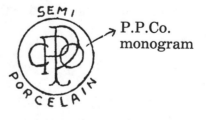

P.P.Co. monogram

(1890-1899)

P.P.Co. monogram

(1890-1904)

(1889, 1890)

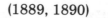

139. Pfaltzgraff Pottery   early 1800s to the present
York, Pa.

> The early products of this company do not fit the scope of this book. They made no early whiteware.

140. Philadelphia City Pottery   1868-c.1910
Philadelphia, Pa.

(c.1900)

> This company was also called J.E. Jeffords & Co. Note the J.E.J.Co. monogram on the mark to the left.

141. Phoenix Pottery   1867-1894
Phoenixville, Pa.

> Phoenix Pottery is best known for Etruscan Majolica made between 1880 and 1890. Most wares are marked with an impressed ETRUSCAN MAJOLICA. On uncolored wares the mark is ETRUSCAN IVORY. A G.S.H. monogram was also used alone. Some majolica pieces were marked only with a letter (A to O) followed by a number.

(Griffen, Smith & Hill)   G.S.H.
monogram

142. Albert Pick   c.1900-c.1950

> Pick was a distributor, not a manufacturer. His mark will be on wares made by other companies. Barber listed this one early mark used before 1904.

143. Pickard China
Chicago, Ill.

1894 to the present

Until the 1930s Pickard used primarily imported European (mostly French) porcelain to be hand-decorated by his fine artists. It is not American porcelain; however, since the *early* decorators were Americans, I've listed these early marks used before 1900.

144. Pioneer Pottery Co.
Wellsville, Ohio

1885-c.1902

Financial problems led the Pioneer Pottery Co. to be reorganized as the Wellsville Pioneer Pottery in 1896. About 1902 it became the Wellesville China Co. continuing until c.1960.

Pioneer Pottery marks used between 1885 and 1896:

The ribbon at the bottom of the above mark may have the words LABOR OMNIA VINCIT.

PIONEER POTTERY

WORKS.

See p. 90 for a mark of a much later Pioneer Pottery Co.

Wellsville Pioneer Pottery marks used from 1896 to c.1902:

144. Pioneer Pottery (continued)

Wellsville China Co. was a continuation of the Wellsville Pioneer Pottery. It operated between 1902 and 1960.

(c.1904)

(c.1904)

Special customer order.

(c.1910-c.1920)

(c.1915-c.1920)

(1920s)

W.C.CO.

DeSoto China and Wellsville China (without Co.) date from the 1930s and later.

145. Pope-Gosser China Co. Coshocton, Ohio

1903-1929; 1933-1958

(c.1905)

THE POPE-GOSSER CHINA CO. SEMI-VITREOUS

(c.1910)

POPE-GOSSER CHINA

The mark to the left was found on a 1909 calendar plate.

(c.1920)

POPE-GOSSER U.S.A.

POPE-GOSSER · CHINA · MADE IN U.S.A.

The mark at left was used from the 1920s to the 1940s.

146. Porcelier Manufacturing Co. Greensburg, Pa.

late 1920s to the 1950s

They made vitrified whiteware; it is not early but is quite collectible. The word PORCELIER is on all the marks.

147. Prospect Hill Pottery Trenton, N.J.

1875-1894

From 1875 to 1880 the company was under Isaac Davis alone. From 1880 to 1894 it was under Dale and Davis and called the Prospect Hill Pottery.

(over for marks)

62

147. Prospect Hill Pottery (continued)

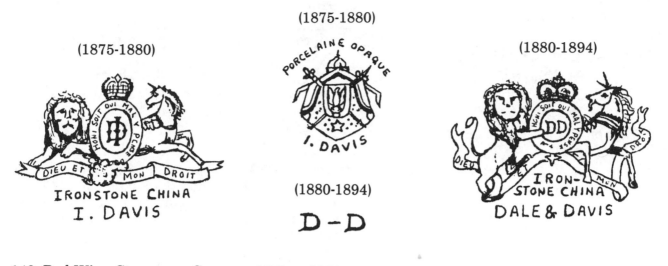

(1875-1880)

(1875-1880)

IRONSTONE CHINA
I. DAVIS

PORCELAINE OPAQUE
I. DAVIS

(1880-1894)

D-D

(1880-1894)

IRON-STONE CHINA
DALE & DAVIS

148. Red Wing Stoneware Co.
Red Wing, Minn.

1870s-c.1970

This company did not make whiteware until the 1920s and particularly the 1930s.

149. Paul Revere Pottery
Boston, Mass.

early 1900s-1940s

They made art pottery primarily. See Paul Evans' *Art Pottery of the United States* for more about this pottery and its marks.

150. Robinson, Ransbottom Pottery Co.
Roseville, Ohio

1920 to at least 1985

Prior to the 1920s they made stoneware. The initials R.R.P. Co. and the word Roseville are often used on their marks and confused with wares made by the Roseville Pottery Co. See Lois Lehner's *Complete Book of American Kitchen and Dinner Wares* for more about this company and its marks.

151. Rookwood Pottery Co.

famous art pottery; marks well-documented

152. Roseville Pottery Co.

primarily art pottery; see other sources for marks

153. Royal China Co.
Sebring, Ohio

1933 to the present

154. Salem China Co.
Salem, Ohio

1898-1967

Jo Cunningham in her book *The Collector's Encyclopedia of American Dinnerware* says that this company was fairly inactive and financially troubled until 1918 when F.A. Sebring took over. Barber, in his 1904 marks book, fails to mention the company at all. This leads me to believe that little was produced or marked by Salem until after the 1918 Sebring takeover. Most Salem ware dates from the 1930s or later. See p. 98 for an early Salem mark.

(over for marks)

154. Salem China Co. (continued)

(c.1910)

SALEM CHINA CO.
SALEM,OHIO

(c.1920)

SALEM
S-V
CHINA

(late 1920s)

ANTIQUE
IVORY
FROM
SALEM
Pat. 1-9-27

155. Saxon China Co.
Sebring, Ohio

c.1900-1929

Gates and Ormerod give 1911 as the beginning date for this company. Lehner says Jervis mentioned the Saxon China Co. as being involved with a merger in 1907, indicating an even earlier founding date. The items I have seen with the first mark below appear to be c.1900 ware.

(c.1900-c.1910)

SAXON
CHINA

(1920s)

156. E.H. Sebring China Co.
Sebring, Ohio

1908-1929

E.H.S.C. Co.
S.V.
CHINA

(1910?)

BELLVIEW
E.H.S.C. Jul 28,10

The Gates and Ormerod mark at left was published in *Historical Archaeology* Vol. 16, Numbers 1 & 2, p.240.

157. Sebring Pottery Co.

See American Pottery Works, no. 11, on p. 13.

158. Sevres China Co.
East Liverpool, Ohio

1900-1908

SÉVRES
HOTEL CHINA

SÉVRES

MELTON

BERLIN

GENEVA

Gates and Ormerod say BELMAR was also used with the mark at left.

64

158. Sevres China Co. (continued)

Don't confuse American Sevres with French Sevres porcelain! Some dealers seem to take monetary advantage from this confusion; or they are just ignorant.

Warner-Keffer China Co.   1908-1911

Warner-Keffer was a contination of the Sevres China Co. in East Liverpool, Ohio. The following marks are from *The East Liverpool, Ohio, Pottery District* by William C. Gates, Jr. and Dana E. Ormerod.*

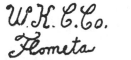 

159. Shenango China (or Pottery) Co.   1901 to the present
New Castle, Pa.

This company had many early problems, including a c.1905 reorganization. The names was changed to Shenango Pottery Co.; however, Shenango China with New Castle, Pa. is used on many later marks. Most Shenango wares will date from after WWI.

(c.1902)

(c.1910)

MADE BY
SHENANGO POTTERY CO
NEW CASTLE, PA.

160. Smith, Fife & Co.   c.1830
Philadelphia, Pa.

They made an early porcelain somewhat inferior to Tucker's. It is very rare.

161. Smith-Phillips China Co.   1901-1929
East Liverpool, Ohio

These first five marks are all Barber (pre-1904) marks. They were used from 1902 to c.1915.

FENIX   AMERICAN GIRL   KOSMO

Smith Phillips Semi Porcelain   This Smith-Phillips mark at left was also used after 1915.

* These Gates and Ormerod marks were published in *Historical Archaeology* Volume 16, Numbers 1 & 2, p.242.

161. Smith-Phillips China Co. (continued)

(c.1910-c.1915)

This mark was used from 1902 to the 1920s; however, MADE IN U.S.A. was not added until c.1920. Some dating was used before 1915 but didn't become common until the 1920s. This mark is for 1921.

(c.1918)

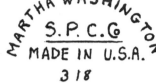
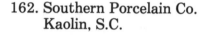

(1920s)

(1920s)

SMITH-PHILLIPS
CHINA
PRINCESS
5-25   (1925)

162. Southern Porcelain Co.
Kaolin, S.C.

1856-c.1875.

Barber said they made a small amount of fine white china and Parian between 1856 and 1862. During the Civil War they made brown stoneware telegraph insulators *impressed* with the mark to the left. Other wares may have been so marked. Ascribe no other marks to this company.

163. Steubenville Pottery Co.
Steubenville, Ohio

1879-1959

The first seven marks below were shape or pattern marks used between 1890 and 1895, according to Barber. The ironstone china marks date from the 1880s to c.1904. Canton China marks date from 1890 to after 1904.

(over for more marks)

163. Steubenville Pottery Co. (continued)

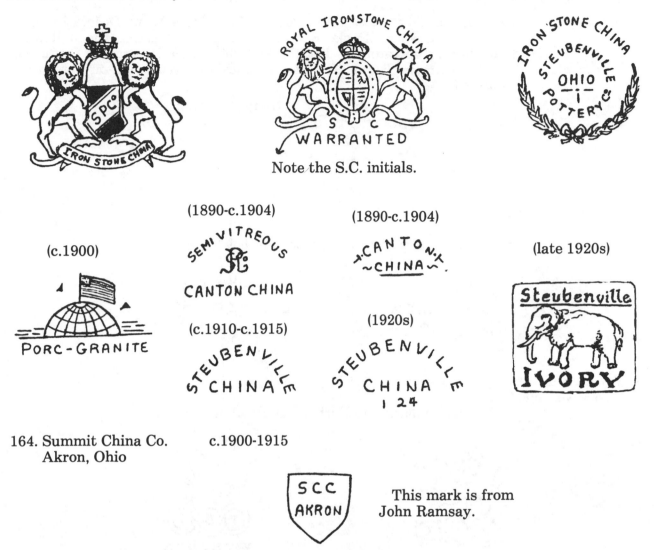

Note the S.C. initials.

(c.1900)

(1890-c.1904)

SEMI VITREOUS
CANTON CHINA

(1890-c.1904)

+CANTON.N.T
~CHINA~.

(late 1920s)

PORC-GRANITE

(c.1910-c.1915)

STEUBENVILLE
CHINA

(1920s)

STEUBENVILLE
CHINA
1 24

Steubenville
IVORY

164. Summit China Co.   c.1900-1915
     Akron, Ohio

S C C
AKRON

This mark is from
John Ramsay.

165. Syracuse China Co.   See Onondaga Pottery, no. 132, on p. 57.

166. Syracuse, N.Y.; Robineau Pottery   c.1903-1920s

Adelaide Alsop-Robineau developed a true hard-paste porcelain of excellent quality. For more about this art porcelain and other early art porcelain, see Paul Evans' *Art Pottery of the United States*. Barber recorded that Adelaide Robineau decorated hotel ware for the Onondaga Pottery Co., and these wares are marked as given here.

A-R

167. Tatler Decorating Co.   c.1876-c.1905
     Trenton, N.J.

Elijah Tatler was a famous decorator both in the United States and England. Just before his death in 1876 he established his own decorating business. His son, W.H. Tatler, continued the business as the W.H. Tatler Decorating Co. Besides Tatler, Barber listed the following decorators as

167. Tatler Decorating Co. (continued)

operating in Trenton in 1893: Pope & Lee, Jesse Dean Decorating Co., W.H. Hendrickson, Poole & Stockton. Barber listed the following decorators as operating in Trenton in 1904: Tatler Decorating Co., Jesse Dean, and George Tunnicliffe, whose names are often found on wares they decorated.

(c.1900-c.1905)

168. Taylor, Lee & Smith Co.   1899-1901
     East Liverpool, Ohio
          This company preceded the Taylor, Smith & Taylor Co.

169. Taylor, Smith & Taylor Co.   1901-1970s
     East Liverpool, Ohio
          These two marks are Barber (pre-1904) marks.

VITREOUS

Gates and Ormerod list the above marks, and one with TAYLOR SMITH & TAYLOR CO. printed under the mark as being in use from 1901 to c.1930. I can't confirm or deny this; however, I doubt they were used commonly beyond c.1910. I have seen many Taylor, Smith & Taylor marks, but I have seen these marks only a few times, always on c.1900-1910 ware. Had they been used until 1930, I believe they would be more commonly seen.

The following Taylor, Smith & Taylor marks date from c.1910 to the 1930s.

(c.1910)

CHINA

(c.1915)

T. S. T.
VERONA
CHINA

(c.1920)

Gates and Ormerod show a different PENNOVA mark.

169. Taylor, Smith & Taylor Co. (continued)

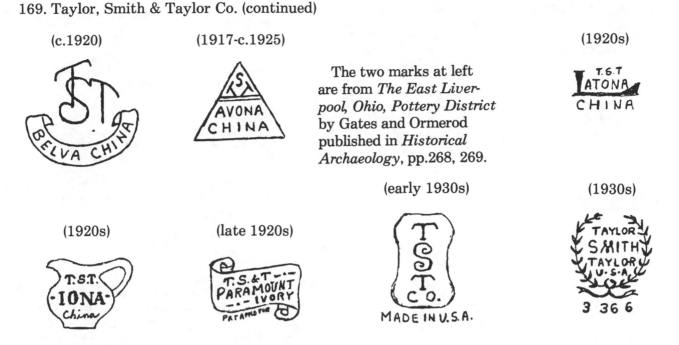

(c.1920)

(1917-c.1925)

The two marks at left are from *The East Liverpool, Ohio, Pottery District* by Gates and Ormerod published in *Historical Archaeology*, pp.268, 269.

(1920s)

(early 1930s)

(1930s)

(1920s)

(late 1920s)

Various wreath marks were used in the 1930s and later. CAPITOL IVORY was used in the 1930s. VISTOSA dates at c.1940. MADE IN U.S.A. was first used c.1930.

170. Tempest, Brockmann & Sampson Pottery Co.   See no.26 on p. 17.

171. Thomas China Co.   c.1904
     Lisbon, Ohio

Thomas China Co.

172. C.C. Thompson Pottery Co.   1889-1938
     East Liverpool, Ohio

This company was called C.C. Thompson & Co. before 1889.

(c.1890-c.1910)

(c.1890-c.1910 for these three marks)

LELAND.   OREGON.

SYDNEY.

69

172. C.C. Thompson Pottery Co. (continued)

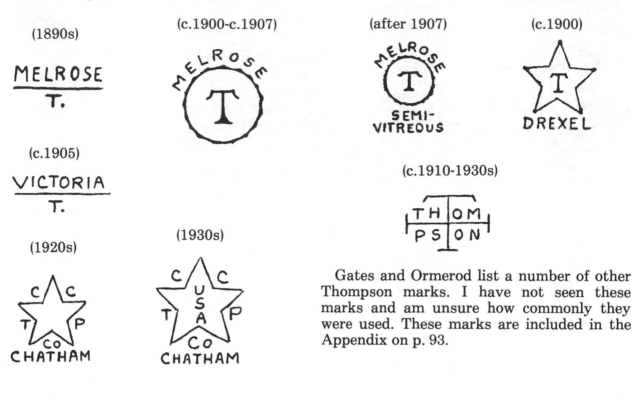

(1890s)

MELROSE
T.

(c.1900-c.1907)

(after 1907)

SEMI-
VITREOUS

(c.1900)

DREXEL

(c.1905)

VICTORIA
T.

(c.1910-1930s)

THOMPSON

(1920s)

CHATHAM

(1930s)

CHATHAM

Gates and Ormerod list a number of other Thompson marks. I have not seen these marks and am unsure how commonly they were used. These marks are included in the Appendix on p. 93.

173. Trenle China Co.
East Liverpool, Ohio

c.1910-c.1935

The Trenle China Co. is a continuation of the East End Pottery Co. For a short time before 1910 the company was called the East End China Co. I found two identical 1910 calendar plates; one was marked E.E.P. Co. (See p. 28.); the other was marked E.E.C. Co. (See below). In the mid-1930s Trenle moved to Ravenswood, W.Va. Here the company became Trenle, Blake China Co.

(c.1909)

Trenle took over the East End China Co. in 1909 but the name wasn't changed until 1910 or 1911.

(1910-c.1920)

(c.1920-c.1935)

TRENLE
CHINA

Trenle ware marked VITRIFIED CHINA date from c.1920 to c.1935.

174. Trenton China Co.
Trenton, N.J.

1859-1891

Barber said they made a fine grade of vitrified china, white and decorated. Their mark given below was *impressed* on wares.

TRENTON CHINA CO.
TRENTON N.J.

175. Trenton Pottery Co.   1865-1870
     Trenton, N.J.

T. P. Co.
CHINA

printed in black
on white granite

Note: Barber listed this mark exactly the same for the Trenton Potteries Co. and dated 1891. In that case the mark was on porcelain dinner ware.

176. Trenton Potteries Co.   1892-c.1960
     Trenton, N.J.

This company was formed from 5 (later 6) companies, of which the Crescent Pottery was the most prominent. On some wares these companies continued to use their original names. The Trenton Potteries made sanitary ware primarily.

(1891)

T. P. Co.
CHINA

Barber credited the Crescent Pottery as using the above mark in 1891, indicating that they led in the formation of the Trenton Potteries Co. See no.175 above for an identical mark.

(1892-c.1904)   (1892-c.1904)   (1896)

(1892-c.1904)   (1902-c.1904)   (1920s or later)

The mark to the left may also have a 3, 4, or 5 in the center.

177. Trenton Pottery Works   c.1875
     Trenton, N.J.

178. William Ellis Tucker   1820s and 1830s
     American China Manufactory
     Philadelphia, Pa.

                      Tucker was an early maker of true porcelain. His ware is famous and well-documented. There is probably no "unaccounted for" Tucker porcelain to be found.

179. Tuxedo Pottery Co.   1902
     Phoenixville, Pa.

                      Barber said they made semi-granite, colored glaze ware and flow blue. Apparently they did not use any marks.

180. Union Porcelain Works   c.1860-c.1904
     Greenpoint, N.Y.

                      They made true hard porcelain. The owners were Thomas C. Smith and his son. They first marked their porcelain in 1876.

(1876)

impressed on
porcelain
tableware

(1877)

printed in
green under
the glaze

                      The next three marks are decorating shop marks. They are above the glaze, usually in red. Sometimes they are dated.

(1879-1891)   (1879-1891)   (1891-1904)

181. Union Potteries Co.   1894-1904
     E. Liverpool, O. & Pittsburgh, Pa.

           The mark at right is from *The East Liverpool, Ohio, Pottery District* by William C. Gates, Jr. & Dana E. Ormerod. Note the U.P. Co. monogram in center of shield.*

* This Gates and Ormerod mark was published in *Historical Archaeology* Volume 16, Numbers 1 & 2, p.297.

181. Union Potteries Co. (continued)

The mark above may
have CARNATION
instead of CORINNE.

182. United States Pottery   c.1850-1858 (for whiteware)
Bennington, Vt.

This company made hard-paste porcelain, among many other
things. They were best known for Parian and Rockingham
wares, some made prior to 1850. The earlier marks included Norton, Fenton, Lyman and Bennington, Vt. Barber said the marks
below were used c.1850 or later. The mark to the right was used
on porcelain and semi-porcelain; however, apparently most was
not marked at all.

Barber said the United States Pottery closed in 1858.

   The raised mark
at left was used
on Parian ware;
various numbers
are on the mark.

impressed on
porcelain or
semi-porcelain

183. United States Pottery Co.   c.1904
East Liverpool, Ohio

This may be a rare case where Barber made a mistake. Gates
and Ormerod found no evidence that this company ever existed
in East Liverpool. This is probably the same company listed
below as being in Wellsville, Ohio. The three marks here are from
Barber's 1904 marks book.

184. United States Pottery Co.   1899-1900; 1907-c.1930
Wellsville, Ohio

This company helped organize the East Liverpool Potteries in
1900. This consolidated company included the United States
Pottery Co., Globe Pottery, Wallace & Chetwynd Pottery, East

73

184. United States Pottery Co. (continued)

Liverpool Pottery, George C. Murphy Pottery, and the East End Pottery. East Liverpool Potteries lost all its member companies in 1903, except the United States Pottery and Globe Pottery. In 1907 these two split and the East Liverpool Potteries ended; however, *the mark did not.* Gates and Ormerod say that the United States Pottery continued alone until c.1930. They marked their ware as though the East Liverpool Potteries was still a reality. These misleading marks are included here.

(c.1899)

(c.1907-c.1920)

EAST LIVERPOOL
POTTERIES CO.

(1920s)

ELPCO
MADE IN U.S.A.
CHINA
4 28

185. Vodrey & Brother;
    Vodrey Pottery Co.
    East Liverpool, Ohio

1857-1896
1896-c.1929

These Vodrey & Brother marks date from 1879 (Barber) to 1896. Gates and Ormerod use 1876 as beginning date.

185. Vodrey Pottery Co. (continued)
     These Vodrey marks date from 1896 to the 1920s.

(1896-c.1910)

KEYSTONE
I

(1896-c.1910)

ADMIRAL
V. P. CO.

(1896-c.1910)

SEMI PORCELAIN

(1896-c.1910)

HOTEL
V. P. CO.

(c.1905-c.1920)

VODREY

CHINA

(c.1905-c.1920)

VERONA
V. P. CO.

(c.1905-c.1920)

BONITA
V. P. CO.

(after c.1910)

VODREY
S - V
CHINA

186. Wallace & Chetwynd Pottery Co.   1881-1900
     East Liverpool, Ohio

SEMI-VITREOUS
W&C CO.
TRADEMARK
OPAQUE CHINA

WALLACE & CHETWYND
W
IRON STONE

TRADE MARK

W. & C.   P. CO.

OPAQUE CHINA

The middle mark below is from
*The East Liverpool, Ohio, Pottery
District* by William C. Gates, Jr.
and Dana E. Ormerod.*

W.&C.P.Co
CHINA

WALLACE & CHETWYND
IRON STONE

OPAQUE
W&C
CHINA

* This Gates and Ormerod mark was published in *Historical Archaeology* Volume 16, Numbers 1 & 2, p.308.

187. Wannopee Pottery Co.   See New Milford Pottery Co. on p. 55.

188. Warwick China Co.   1887-1951
Wheeling, W.Va.

(1892-c.1904)

(1893-1898)

The ribbon under the mark at left may have W.C. Co. instead of Warwick China Co. after c.1905.

WARWICK
SEMI
PORCELAIN

(1898-c.1910)

WARWICK
CHINA

(c.1905-c.1920)

IOGA

(1920s)

The mark at left had MADE IN U.S.A. added in the 1930s. Later marks were also dated.

189. Weller Pottery   c.1890-1948
Zanesville, Ohio

Apparently Weller made little but art pottery before World War I. Kitchen ware was made from the 1920s on. The word WELLER is on all or nearly all Weller products.

190. Wellsville China Co.   See Pioneer Pottery on pp. 61 and 62.

191. West End Pottery Co.   1893-1938
East Liverpool, Ohio

(1893-c.1910)

CUBAN
W.E.P. Co.

PURITAN
W.E.P. CO.
E.L.O.

The two marks at left date c.1915.

(1893-c.1910)

W.E.P CO.
CHINA

W.E.P. CO.
VITREOUS
HOTEL CHINA

191. West End Pottery Co. (continued)

(1920s)

WEST END

(1930s)

192. Western Stoneware Co.
Monmouth, Ill.

1906 to the present

Despite its name, this company apparently made some whiteware from the very beginning (or a stoneware that looked like whiteware). See Lois Lehner's *Complete Book of American Kitchen and Dinner Wares* for more about this company.

193. Wheeling Pottery Co.
Wheeling Potteries
Wheeling, W.Va.

1879-1903
1903-1909 or 1910

The La Belle Pottery was formed in 1887 as a part of the Wheeling Pottery Co. The well-known La Belle flow blue was made here.

(1880-1886)

(1880-1886)

THE WHEELING STONE CHINA POTTERY CO.

(1880-1886)

(1886-1896)

(1896-c.1904)

(1888-1893)

193. Wheeling Pottery Co. (continued)

(1888-1893) (1888-1893) (1893-c.1904) (1893-c.1904)

(1894-1904; possibly 1909) (c.1904-c.1909)

THE
WHEELING
POTTERY
CO.

I found this mark on a
commemorative piece dated
1907. It was printed in
gold. A gold mark is rare
for early American
whiteware.

Barber did not date these next 4 marks; however, he did say
they were being used in 1904, the year of his marks book.

The AVON mark was used after 1903 by the
Wheeling Potteries Co. Other marks remained un-
changed after the 1903 reorganization.

194. Whitmore, Robinson & Co. 1862-c.1888
     Akron, Ohio

They made an imitation whiteware. It was buff-colored ware
covered with an opaque white glaze. It was probably not
marked.

195. Wick China Co. 1889-c.1905
     Kittanning, Pa.

This company became the Pennsylvania China or Pottery Co.
from c.1905 to 1913. The second mark below is from John Ramsay. His marks are often quite inaccurate. The actual mark may

195. Wick China Co. (continued)

be identical to the Wick mark at left except for the monogram in the center. Ramsay mistakenly attributed the mark to the Pioneer Pottery Co.

(c.1890-c.1905)　　　　　　　　(c.1905-1913)

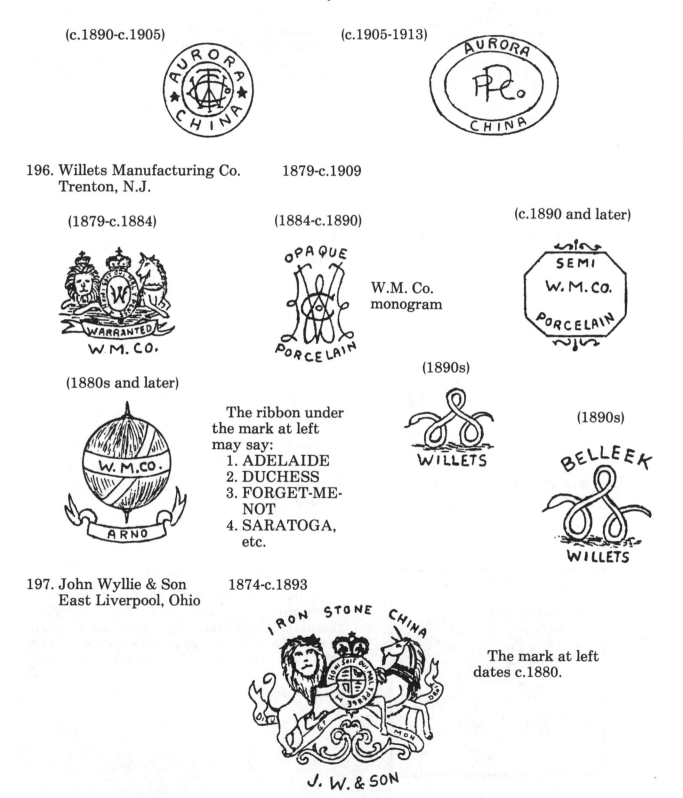

196. Willets Manufacturing Co.　　1879-c.1909
Trenton, N.J.

(1879-c.1884)　　　(1884-c.1890)　　　　　　(c.1890 and later)

W.M. Co.
monogram

(1880s and later)　　　　　　　　　　　　(1890s)

The ribbon under
the mark at left
may say:
　1. ADELAIDE
　2. DUCHESS
　3. FORGET-ME-
　　NOT
　4. SARATOGA,
　　etc.

(1890s)

197. John Wyllie & Son　　1874-c.1893
East Liverpool, Ohio

The mark at left
dates c.1880.

79

197. John Wyllie & Son (continued)

(after 1880)

This mark is an elaboration of the unique two shields (American and English) mark. See the Appendix, p. 96, for a brief history of the mark. Unlike the other companies that used this mark, I find no special reason, other than the fact that John Wyllie was from England, for the Wyllie company to have used this mark.

198. H.R. Wyllie China Co.   c.1910-c.1929
     Huntington, W.Va.

The mark at left dates c.1920.

199. William Young & Sons   1853-1870
     William Young's Sons   1870-1879
     Trenton, N.J.

(c.1870-1879)

Barber said the company used an eagle mark in 1858; however, he did not picture the mark. He said that they used an English mark (shown here) from 1858 to 1879. The W Y S on the mark at left probably indicates it was used after 1870. W.Y. & Sons may be on the earlier mark.

APPENDIX

Miscellaneous American Marks

The marks included in the Appendix are those that for one reason or another need special explanation. Some are old American marks whose company of manufacture is in doubt. Some are marks I believe may be exceedingly rare. Some present unique problems, and a few others are just marks discovered too late to be included in the main section.

A.1

NYCP

A.2

These first two marks from John Ramsay were listed for the New York City Pottery. Ramsay's marks are usually quite simplified. Some seem to be drawn from memory, resulting in inevitable mistakes. This can be seen by comparing marks that both he and Barber included in their books. See pp. 55 and 56 for marks of the New York City Pottery.

A.3

(British mark)

Ramsay listed this mark as being for the Anchor Pottery Co. of Trenton, N.J. Barber had no marks for this company with A.P. initials. See p. 14. However, the Anchor Porcelain Co. of Staffordshire, England, did use initials with their anchor mark. If the ware in question is true porcelain, the mark would probably be for the English company. If the ware is common whiteware, the mark would likely be for the Anchor Pottery Co. of the U.S., probably dating from after 1904. Keep in mind: Ramsay's marks are usually quite simplified and the actual anchor mark may be more than a little different from this mark.

A.4

C.C.T.

John Ramsay listed this mark for the C.C. Thompson Pottery Co. I doubt the validity of this mark but felt that it should at least be included in the Appendix.

81

A.5

perhaps c.1907

This mark from John Ramsay for the International Pottery Co. is possibly a mistake. Barber showed an almost identical mark and many similar marks with Burgess & Campbell. See p. 38. There was a Burroughs & Mountford Co. in operation at the same time in Trenton. If this mark is correct, it would indicate some company combination for Burgess and Mountford after c.1903. According to Barber, the Burroughs & Mountford Co. operated until at least 1893 but was out of operation when he published his marks book in 1904. The International Pottery Co. continued well after 1904. Mountford may have joined that company. This would fit well with Barber's information that John A. Campbell left the International Pottery Co. as an owner in 1904 but remained as company treasurer until 1906 (date from Lois Lehner) when he joined the Trenton Potteries Co. Therefore, if this is a true mark, it seems unlikely that William Burgess would have used Mountford's name as part of his mark until after 1906 when his old friend, John Campbell, left the company completely.

A.6

Ramsay illustrated this mark for Thomas Maddock & Sons. Barber showed a similar mark. This is likely a true, if simplified, Maddock mark. See p. 46. I can find no British company that this mark could represent. Remember: Ramsay's marks are often simplified and the actual mark may be different from the one at left. Any anchor mark with T.M.&S. is probably for Thomas Maddock & Sons Co.

A.7

$$\mathcal{H} \quad \phi \quad \mathcal{G}$$

$$d\phi \quad \mathcal{F}d$$

(incised)

Ramsay illustrated these incised marks for porcelain from the Columbian Art Pottery Co. of Morris and Willmore in Trenton, N.J. Since this company made much art pottery, these marks were probably artists' signatures and they may have accompanied the company's shield mark used on belleek ware. See p. 23. These marks may never have been used alone. Barber made no mention of such incised marks for this company.

A.8

I first saw this mark for the Akron China Co. after the main section of the book had been completed. See p. 11.

A.9

This mark is for the International Pottery Co. of Trenton, N.J. About 1903 this company was using a similar mark with BURGESS & CO. instead of INTERNATIONAL under the mark. See p. 38. In 1903 John Campbell withdrew his share of ownership of the company and his name was removed from the various company marks. The name of William Burgess was probably dropped from company marks after he left the company. The mark dates from c.1910 to c.1920.

A.10

This mark is a fairly common early American mark. It may be for the Empire Pottery of Trenton, N.J. In 1892 this company joined the Trenton Potteries Co. along with several other companies. Some kept a separate identity apart from the Trenton Potteries; most continued to about WWI. However, I believe the mark is from an Ohio pottery. Lois Lehner says it is an old Steubenville Pottery mark but does not elaborate or provide documentation. I can't confirm or deny her contention.* Every Empire China mark I have seen has been in gold. This is rare for early American marks but not unique. The Wheeling Pottery Co. used gold marks in the early years of this century. Whatever its company, it is an early American mark dating from c.1905 to c.1915.

A.11

This mark from C. Jordan Thorn is for the Cook Pottery Co. of Trenton, N.J. Barber said this three-feathers mark was used by the Cook Pottery on belleek ware. He pictured the three feathers mark with just the word ETRURIA on the ribbon. He also pictured it with MELLOR & CO. under the ribbon. This mark with CH.H.C. initials would date to the same period — c.1904 or earlier. The initials are for Charles Howell Cook, the president of the company. Mellor (a partner to Cook) & Co. was used on most ware to prevent confusion with the Cook and Hancock mark of the older Crescent Pottery that Charles Howell Cook had organized with W.H. Hancock in 1881. The Cook Pottery Co. did use the Cook name or initials on a few "special" products. COOK POTTERY CO., TRENTON, N.J. was used on later marks.

* Just prior to publication, I found a piece with this mark *and* a c.1910 Steubenville mark.

A.12

This mark was used on Delft-type ware made by the Cook Pottery Co. of Trenton, N.J. See p.23. Except for the addition of D.C., this mark is an identical copy of the bottle mark used on Delft produced in the 19th century. This mark, without the word Delft, was used many years before but was being used again on Delft ware made in Holland in the middle to late 1800s. Cook was certainly aware of this newer Delft. He was probably trying to make his own form of it. The D.C. could stand for Delft-Cook or possibly a family member (his wife?) who helped him on the project. Barber considered Cook's Delft ware to be the best imitation of Delft made in this country. Barber said Cook's Delft was made in 1897.

A.13

I found this old Barber mark on a plate commemorating the 50th anniversary (1854-1904) of Atlantic City. This mark was used by the Cook Pottery Co. Mellor was a partner to Cook. See p. 23. Barber did note date the various Cook marks, but the anniversary plate would indicate the mark shown here was used c.1904. I have seen this mark on many whiteware items, indicating that it was probably used for quite a few years. Based on the whiteware marked, I would date the mark c.1900 to c.1910.

A.14

c.1895-c.1900

The outline of this mark is identical to one pictured by Barber on a special jug made to commemorate Admiral Dewey's victory at Manila. This Barber mark included the date of patent, 1899.

This mark is for the Cook Pottery Co. of Trenton, N.J. Mellor was a partner of Cook. The number below the mark was apparently used to make it look like an English Registry Number. The only other American company to use such numbers, as far as I know, was the Crescent Pottery, of which Cook was a founder along with W.S. Hancock.

A.15

COOK POTTERY CO.
TRENTON, N.J.

This simple mark was used by the Cook Pottery from c.1910 to c.1920.

A.16

IRONSTONE CHINA
W. B. S. & Co.

c.1878

This mark was found on a platter with a nice moss rose decoration. It is for the William Brunt, Son & Co. of East Liverpool, Ohio. See p. 17. Gates and Ormerod show similar marks for the William Brunt Jr. & Co. (W.B. Jr. & Co.) that preceded the William Brunt, Son & Co. in 1877 and 1878. William Brunt, Son & Co. dated from 1878 to c.1894. This transition mark would date c.1878.

A.17

I found this mark on an old whiteware umbrella holder. I mistakenly believed it to be a mark for the Chester Pottery Co. Gates and Ormerod show it to be for the Taylor, Smith & Taylor Co. The name comes from the fact that the company had a factory in Chester, W.Va. Earlier marks will have no numbers under the mark; later marks will have numbers indicating the date. Gates and Ormerod say the mark was used between 1908 and c.1930.

A.18

Columbia Chinaware was a mark used by the Harker Pottery Co. from circa World War I through the 1930s. The mark at left was used in the 1920s. A mark that included ESTABLISHED 1873 was used in the 1930s.

A.19

c.1900-c.1910

I found this mark on a portrait plate. It would date c.1910 or a bit earlier. Unfortunately, there are several companies this mark could represent. Several used C.P. Co. initials on their mark; however, the most likely company to have used this mark was the Crown Pottery Co. of Evansville, Ind.

A.20

5-26

This is a 1920s mark for the Southern Potteries Inc. of Erwin, Tenn. This company operated from 1918 to the 1950s.

A.21 c.1920

STERLING
Hiawatha
PORCELAIN

A.22 1920s

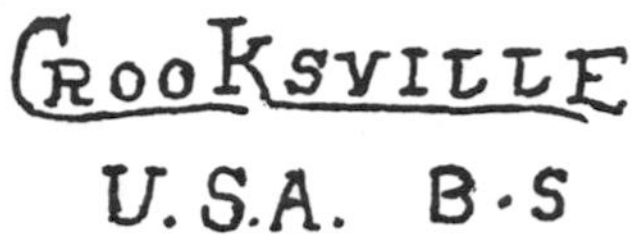

CROOKSVILLE
U.S.A. B·S

A.23 1930s

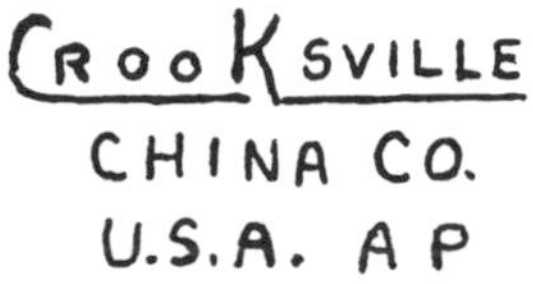

CROOKSVILLE
CHINA CO.
U.S.A. AP

A.24 1930s

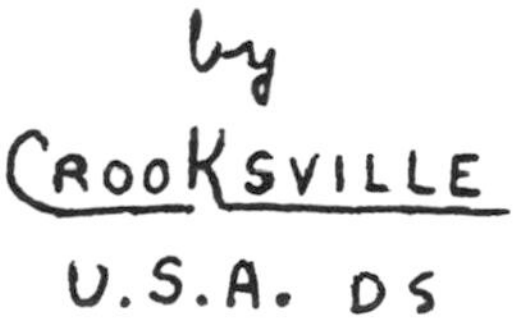

by
CROOKSVILLE
U.S.A. DS

A.25 c.1930

Provincial Ware

(often on ware with chrome frame)

CROOKSVILLE CHINA COMPANY

The Crooksville China Co. operated in Crooksville, Ohio, between 1902 and 1959. They used numerous marks over the years. However, I have had a disconcertingly difficult time dating their marks. There needs to be more research on this company and its marks. My current thinking is that, probably due to internal company problems between c.1910 and the early 1920s, little was produced by this company prior to the 1920s. I have included most of the Crooksville marks here in the Appendix because I feel that there may need to be some additional revision in the dating of these marks.

STERLING PORCELAIN was made by Crooksville, some dating back to c.1910. See mark on p. 25. The STERLING PORCELAIN mark shown here probably dates c.1920. The Crooksville China Co. made STINTHAL CHINA which had many marks, some including C.C. Co. initials or monograms. Stinthal dates from c.1910 to 1920 and probably later. There is a small chance they also used a STERLING CHINA mark. See p. 92 for a discussion about STERLING CHINA marks.

The later Crooksville marks shown here should be dated fairly accurately; however, I keep finding marks with slight variations from those illustrated here. These variations may indicate some difference in the dates when the marks were used.

A.26 1930s

PANTRY
BAK-IN
by WARE
Crooksville

A.27 1930s and later

CROOKSVILLE
CHINA Co,
H-N
MADE IN U.S.A.

A.28 1940s

CROOKSVILLE
CHINA Co.

A.29

CHELSEA

This is a Taylor, Smith & Taylor Co. mark from the 1930s. It is sometimes found without T.S.T. initials, making it difficult to identify.

A.30

This mark must be for the East Palestine Pottery Co.; however the mark is unusual and quite different from the earlier company mark. See p. 30. The mark would date from after 1905 to 1909.

A.31

Eureka

I found this mark on a bowl that would date c.1910. Gates and Ormerod show two Eureka marks they ascribe to the C.C. Thompson Pottery Co. dating c.1915. The mark shown here is different from the Gates and Ormerod marks but it may be for the same company. In any case, they date about the same time.

A.32

THE GOODWIN POTTERY CO.
SEMI-PORCELAIN

This Goodwin Pottery Co. mark is in the main section of this book. See p. 35. I have added it here for a special reason. What I think makes this mark truly noteworthy is a hidden message. Inside the flower wreath, just to the right of the 1844, is a hidden 93, the actual date for the founding of the Goodwin Pottery Co. This is the kind of thing that makes early American marks so interesting. Some companies used their marks to express humor, to make satirical comment, or to give personal information, as this Goodwin mark does. While wanting to use the date 1844 to recognize the family's earliest attempts at pottery making, they still met their need for historical accuracy by hiding a 93 among the flowers. Note: not all the versions of this mark have a hidden 93.

The practical need for early American whiteware makers to imitate British marks led to considerable creativity in the designing of these marks. While wanting the mark to look superficially British, the Americans' national and personal pride led them to use their marks to subtly, and sometimes not so subtly, satirize the very British marks they were imitating. It is fun trying to discover these devious barbs thrust into the British Lion.

A.33

This Goodwin Pottery Co. mark dates c.1910. Gates and Ormerod show a similar mark with the word USONA.

A.34

This mark and information come from *The East Liverpool, Ohio, Pottery District* by William C. Gates, Jr. and Dana E. Ormerod.* This mark is for Godwin & Flentke of East Liverpool, Ohio. They operated between 1878 and 1880. William Flentke operated alone between 1882 and 1886. He used a similar eagle mark. The G. on the Godwin and Flentke mark may look like a C.

A.35   BEFORE 1920

I believe the following information about the Homer Laughlin Co. will help the collector to quickly distinguish between pre-1920 and post-1920 marks without dealing with the rather complicated and sometimes rather confusing dating system used on early Homer Laughlin marks. Every pre-1920 mark I have seen conforms to the sample mark shown here. Every post-1920 mark conforms to the sample mark shown here. However, since this has involved only about 22 or so marks to date, I am not yet ready to declare the system infallible.

A.36   AFTER 1920

usually with MADE IN U.S.A.

Note the difference between the first L's of the two Laughlins. Also, note the horizontal line connecting the H and C of the monogram. On the earlier mark the line goes through the left vertical line of the H and through the C on the right. It does not on the later mark.

A.37   1970s and later

One Homer Laughlin mark used in the 1970s and later again has an open loop on the first L of Laughlin. However, note the different monogram and the MADE IN U.S.A. not found on early Homer Laughlin marks.

* This Gates and Ormerod mark was published in *Historical Archaeology* Volume 16, Numbers 1 & 2, p. 46.

A.38

This Homer Laughlin Co. mark dates c.1910.

A.39

c.1900

This mark was first used c.1900 by the Maddock Pottery Co. of Trenton, N.J. See p. 46. Although operated by and partly owned by Thomas Maddock & Sons, the Maddock Pottery Co. was a separate company operating out of the old Lamberton Works. The Maddock Pottery Co. became the Scammell China Co. in the middle 1920s. In the 1930s Scammell developed a true porcelain named Lamberton China after the old Maddock Pottery Co. mark shown here. In the 1950s the Scammell China Co. was taken over by the Sterlin China Co. They continued to make Lamberton China. The later Lamberton China marks are easy to distinguish from the early mark. The shield has an S, not an M. A wreath usually surrounds the shield. Below the mark is SCAMMELL or STERLING.

A.40

I don't yet know anything about this mark except that it is old. I found it on a toilet set of five or so pieces. Only the larger pieces were marked. I am sure the set would date back to 1900 or earlier. Based on shape and decoration, I would not be surprised if it dated c.1880.

A.41   c.1900

The next four marks are for the D. E. McNicol Pottery Co. of East Liverpool, Ohio. The marks and dates are from *The East Liverpool, Ohio, Pottery District* by William C. Gates, Jr. and Dana E. Ormerod.* Although I have seen scores of marks for this company, I have not seen any of these marks. I believe they may be rare. Because of this I have relegated them to the Appendix.

A.42   c.1905

* These Gates and Ormerod marks were published in *Historical Archaeology* Volume 16, Numbers 1 & 2, p.187.

A.43   c.1905   D.E. McNicol marks (continued)

A.44   1897-c.1915

A.45

I found this mark on an old basin that would date c.1900 or earlier. I have been unable to identify any Menelik Co.

A.46

Gates and Ormerod say this mark was for Mountford & Co. that operated in East Liverpool, Ohio, between 1891 and 1897.

A.47

◇ C.C̲o̲.

Thorn credited this mark to the Ohio China Co. of East Palestine, Ohio, and well it may be; however, since this isn't a Barber mark, and particularly because the mark is just initials, it could be for another company. There are two prime possibilities: the Oliver China Co. of Sebring, Ohio, or the Owen China Co. of Minerva, Ohio.

A.48

This mark is not for the old Pioneer Pottery of Wellsville, Ohio. It is for a company that operated c.1940 and later.

A.49

This mark was used on porcelain decorated by hand at the Sinclaire Glass Co. of Corning, N.Y. The porcelain blanks were European imports. This experiment at decorating porcelain lasted for a short time in the early 1900s. The dates are c.1902 - c.1920. The mark is probably rare.

A.50

SCAMMELL'S
TRENTON CHINA

These two marks are for the Scammell China Co. of Trenton, N.J. This company operated from the middle 1920s to 1954. For more about the company see p. 89.

A.51

TRENTON CHINA
MADE IN AMERICA

A.52   c.1910-c.1925

STANDARD POTTERY COMPANY

Gates and Ormerod say the Standard Pottery Co. operated from 1886 to 1927 in East Liverpool, Ohio. Barber mentioned the company in his 1893 book but does not include any marks for them in his 1904 book. Gates and Ormerod show one very early mark with an S.C. Co. monogram instead of an S.P. Co. monogram. I believe this mark could be for some other company. See p. 104. The only one of the three marks shown here that I have seen is no. 54. No. 52 and no. 53 are from Gates and Ormerod. Their marks were published in *Historical Archaeology* Volume 16, Number 1 & 2, p.249.

A.53   1920s

ESTHER

A.54   1920s

A.55   c.1900-c.1915

The CO in the base of crown is usually difficult to see. I believe this was intentional.

A.56

The center of this mark is an S.C. Co. monogram.

A.57

Sterling China

This mark may be unrelated to the other two.

The origin of these Sterling China marks is still a mystery. They are not for the Sterling China Co. of Wellsville, Ohio. Although beginning c.1918, they did not operate in a big way until the 1930s. Their marks date from the 1930s to the 1980s. Lehner put the marks shown here with this later Sterling China Co. marks. Gates and Ormerod credited the marks to a Sterling China Co. that was, for a year or so c.1900, the name for the Limoges China Co. of Sebring, Ohio. Based upon the whiteware I had seen with these Sterling China marks (particularly the crown mark), I was certain the marks were in use c.1905 to c.1915 but I could not prove it. If correct, then Lehner as well as Gates and Ormerod had credited the marks to the wrong company.

Fortunately, I recently found a bowl with the portrait of a lady. The portrait was signed COPYRIGHT 1907 BY PHILIP BOILEAU, indicating the bowl was made in that year or soon after. This bowl had the Sterling China crown mark. This information, as well as my previous observations, lead me to date the marks c.1900 to c.1915 or perhaps a bit later. They were probably special marks for some known company. Lamberton China, Kokus China and Canton China are examples of this. What makes these marks different is that two of them have not just Sterling China but also a Co. in a monogram (no. 56) or hidden in the crown (no. 55). This might indicate these marks are for some unknown company; however, I doubt it.

I believe one of these companies may have used the marks listed:

1. Crooksville China Co.
    They made Sterling Porcelain and Stinthal China.

2. Limoges China Co.
    This was the later name of a company first called Sterling China. They may have continued to use Sterling China marks along with their Limoges marks. See p. 46.

3. Standard Pottery Co.
    Gates and Ormerod show an early mark for this company with an S.C. Co. monogram. This company seems to have few other early marks.

4. Steubenville Pottery Co.

A.58

SMITH-PHILLIPS
ALAMO

This Smith-Phillips China Co. mark dates c.1920.

A.59

J.F. STEELE

J.F. Steele was a decorator who worked in East Liverpool, Ohio, in the 1880s. His mark may be found alone or accompanied by the mark of the company that made the whiteware.

A.60

I found this mark on a commemorative piece dated 1904. Both W.H. Tatler and George Tunnicliffe were mentioned by Barber as being Trenton, N.J., decorators in 1904. Tatler had been in business for a long time. See p. 67 for more about the W.H. Tatler Decorating Co. Tunnicliffe was fairly new to the business in 1904. Apparently he had failed as an independent decorator and by 1904 was working for the established Tatler Co. There could be some other explanation for two decorators having marks on a single item but this seems the most plausible.

A.61   c.1920-c.1935

The C.C. Thompson Pottery Co. of East Liverpool, Ohio, has been one of the most troublesome in terms of dating their marks. Fortunately, Barber has provided quite a few Thompson marks proving their being in use in 1904 or earlier. The problems come with the later marks. Gates and Ormerod in their book, *The East Liverpool, Ohio, Pottery District*, provide many later marks for this company including the three marks shown here.* The accompanying dates are also from Gates and Ormerod. Marks no. 61 and no. 62 appear to be of an early style of indicating to me they were in use before 1920. Gates and Ormerod say the Thompson Co. made its first semi-porcelain in 1917. I believe this date is incorrect. (1917 would be very late for a company's instituting the manufacture of semi-porcelain; most did this in the 1890s or the early 1900s.) If the date is changed to 1907, the dating for these marks might be set back ten years. These marks dated ten years earlier are more in keeping with the style of this earlier period. However, it must be stressed, I have no proof of this as yet.

A.62   c.1920-c.1930

A.63   c.1920

THOMPSON
GLENWOOD

* See *Historical Archaeology* Volume 16, Numbers 1 & 2, pp.290-292.

A.64

C.C. Thompson & Co. was the name of the C.C. Thompson Pottery Co. before 1889. This mark was found on a badly damaged bowl. The mark was blurred; however the name was legible. The mark would date in the late 1880s.

A.65

W. C. CO.

(under the knight mark)

Ramsay and Thorn both showed these W.C. Co. initials on the ribbon or banner under the knight-in-armor mark of the Warwick China Co. of Wheeling, W.Va. See p. 76. The early knight mark pictured by Barber had Warwick China Co. on the ribbon. The later mark had just Warwick on the ribbon. These W.C. Co. initials were probably used c.1905 or a bit later.

A.66

The Wheelock Pottery began in the late 1800s in Peoria, Ill., making common utilitarian pottery. I do not know if they ever developed their own whiteware. At some point, probably before 1920, they became importers of foreign wares. This mark is an example of these foreign imports.

A.67

A.68

These two marks are for the Willets Manufacturing Co. of Trenton, N.J. See a similar mark on p. 79. These are really just different versions of the same mark. Barber did not picture the mark, but did describe it as being an octagon-shaped mark used on semi-porcelain ware made at the Willets Co. I have seen the various versions of the mark. Although used before 1904, I suspect this mark was used until c.1909.

A.69

D. & D.

CHINA

I found this mark on a nicely decorated set of bone dishes. The whiteware was of good quality. The mark is for Dale & Davis of the Prospect Hill Pottery of Trenton, N.J. They operated between 1880 and c.1894. Barber said they used only initials on later marks. This mark would date c.1890. See p. 62.

A.70   1913

Thos Maddock's Sons Co.
Trenton, N.J.

(marked on German blank)

Thomas Maddock & Sons became the Thomas Maddock's Sons Co. in 1902. They continued to c.1929. Shortly after 1902 they became a decorating company primarily (possibly exclusively). By 1913 they were importing foreign blanks. They may have been doing this before 1913. If the whiteware used is porcelain it would be imported. Thomas Maddock's Sons Co. may not have made whiteware long after 1902.

A.71   1929

THE
EDWIN M. KNOWLES
IVORY
29-2-11

A.72

WARRANTED
22 K GOLD
HAND DECORATED

Ivory Porcelain by Sebring
REG US PAT OFF
PAT 3-24-1925

CUNNINGHAM
PICKETT DIV.
TROPIC

This mark for the Edwin M. Knowles Co. is typical of the various IVORY marks used c.1929. The Sebring Pottery Co. (American Pottery Works) was probably the first to use an IVORY mark in the 1920s. Their IVORY PORCELAIN was patented in 1925 and continued to be made through the 1930s and possibly even later. The Cunningham and Pickett under the mark at left were retailers or jobbers. They did not make whiteware. For more about Cunningham and Pickett, see Lehner's *Complete Book of American Kitchen and Dinner Wares.*

By the late 1920s most American whiteware companies had a product they marked IVORY, often given a special name such as ROYAL IVORY, etc. Since many companies were dating their marks in the 1920s, the date for a mark can be verified. I have seen dozens of these IVORY marks. By far, the most common date for them is 1929. Since many companies failed in 1929 or soon after, the IVORY mark was often a death knell. Knowles, Taylor and Knowles' IVORY mark is a prime example of this. For companies that survived the Great Depression, IVORY marks continued well into the 1930s.

A.73   c.1929

K.T.& K.
IVORY

A.74

(used in various marks)

The double shield mark is my favorite American (and/or British) mark. The left shield is American; the right one is British. In 1878 or 1879* Edward Clarke (Barber correctly spelled it Clarke in his 1893 book but misspelled it Clark in his 1904 marks book), a potter from Burslem, England, and James Carr from the New York City Pottery jointly organized the Lincoln Pottery Co. at Trenton, N.J., in the old Speeler Works, adopting the double shield mark with Carr and Clarke printed under the

* Barber said 1878 in an earlier book and 1879 in his marks book.

A.75   c.1879

(N.Y. City Pottery mark)

A.76   c.1879

A.77   c.1880

shields. Carr and Clarke were helped by John Moses of Trenton's Glasgow Pottery and his younger brother, James Moses, from the Mercer Pottery also of Trenton, N.J. Just a few months later the partnership ended. Edward Clarke went back to England where, from 1880 to 1887, he used the double shield mark at the Churchyard Works, Burslem. His mark was the same as the Mercer Pottery mark (no. 77) shown here. Under the mark was Edward Clarke / Burslem, England. James Carr returned to the New York City Pottery where he used the double shield mark on cream-colored ware. Barber pictured the Carr double shield mark as using only the words TRADE MARK with the shields.

Carr sold his interest in the company to John Moses, who then proceeded to sell his now half-interest in the company to William Burgess and John A. Campbell. With the leaving of Carr and Clarke, the company became the International Pottery Company in 1879. Burgess and Campbell continued to use the double shield mark with Burgess & Campbell printed under the shields. Edward Clarke sold his interest to Burgess and Campbell at some point. James Moses of the Mercer Pottery Co. may or may not have sold his interest; however, he did remain connected with the company in some way. His Mercer Pottery Co. and the International Pottery Co. of Burgess and Campbell worked together for at least a few years. He used two versions of the double shield mark. One is identical to the Burgess & Campbell mark shown above; the other, shown at left, is identical to the English mark used by Edward Clarke. There must have remained some connection between James Moses and Clarke. It seems more than coincidence that they would use identical marks. In any case, there were five companies using the double shield mark and, except for the short-lived Lincoln Pottery Co., the mark was used at about the same time in both America and England.

To add to this already complicated story, John Wyllie & Son of East Liverpool, Ohio, used the double shield as part of one of their marks; however, since it is an elaboration of the original mark it would most certainly date after the other marks. See p. 80. I do not know why this company used the double shield. Perhaps Mr. Wyllie had some connection with one of the other companies. He was originally from England.

A.78

T.S.T.
VERONA
CHINA
MADE IN U. S. A.
5 10

This mark at left is one of those exceptions that proves the rule. It has me truly perplexed. I found the mark on a nice 1930s-looking (or so I thought!) vegetable tureen. Its lines are sleek and uncluttered. It has a rose decal decoration that is typical of the 1920s and 1930s. Only the heavy-bottomed shape seems to suggest an earlier product.

The mark itself is a total contradiction. The Taylor, Smith and Taylor VERONA CHINA mark dates c.1915. I have seen the mark several times and they did not have MADE IN U.S.A. or numbers under VERONA CHINA. The ware they marked seemed to fit the c.1915 period. Taylor, Smith and Taylor did not generally use MADE IN U.S.A. until the 1930s, yet the numbers under this mark indicate a 1910 date for the mark.

So what do we have?

We have a 1930s-looking tureen with a VERONA CHINA mark (c.1915) with MADE IN U.S.A. (used after 1930 by this company) and a 5-10 indicating probably 1910 as the date of manufacture.

I don't really have an explanation for these contradictions. If the tureen was made in the 1930s, the 5-10 might indicate when VERONA CHINA was first produced at Taylor, Smith and Taylor; however, I doubt this. Weighing the one set of facts against the opposing set, I believe the scales are tipped in favor of the 1910 date. What does the tipping is the 5-10 at the bottom of the mark. I don't believe this particular company would use anything but authentic dates at the bottom of their marks.

A.79

AMERICAN CHINA CO
USA
TORONTO OHIO

If this is a 1910 mark, the MADE IN U.S.A. would be a very early (possibly the earliest) example of the use of this phrase on a mark. The only other early mark that set U.S.A. apart was a c.1905-c.1910 mark for the American China Co. of Toronto, Ohio. This mark is shown at left. All other early marks that had U.S.A. (and they are few) used it as part of a location — for example: East Liverpool, Ohio, U.S.A. The only possible exception is a mark used by the Thomas China Co. of Lisbon, Ohio. Even in this case the U.S.A., although alone, still indicates location.

A.80

F. B. & Co.
F.

This is an English, not American, mark. I included it here, however, because it is the only English mark that fooled me into believing it to be American. I found the mark on a plate in a stack of plates I was checking. They were mostly American — some fairly old. This mark looks

A.80

F. B. & Co.
F.

like a French Limoges mark, but the plate was not porcelain but ordinary whiteware. I recorded the mark as American to be researched later. It is, however, an English mark for Frank Beardmore & Co. of Fenton, England. Although a 20th century product, the word ENGLAND was not a part of the mark. This mark is not typical of the English marks one usually finds in this country.

A.81

NASSAU CHINA Co.
TRENTON, N.J.

I know nothing about this mark. I found it on a very plain white mug of heavy hotel porcelain or semi-porcelain. It could have been made almost any time in this century. I would appreciate information about this company.

A.82

CROOKSVILLE
CHINA CO,
343

This mark is an excellent example of why the Crooksville China Co. is a problem with regard to the dating of its marks. This is definitely a late Crooksville mark. It even included a number under the mark indicating a 1940s date for the piece; however, the whiteware itself (a small pitcher), in both shape and decoration, was made to look like a turn-of-the-century piece.

A.83

SACHCO.

This is an early mark for the Salem China Co. of Salem, Ohio. It would date from c.1900 to c.1910.

A.84

↓
H

This mark is probably for the Harold Pottery Co. of Golden, Colorado. They made chemical and other porcelain between 1910 and c.1914. This mark was found on a mortar with pestle. This company became the Coors Porcelain Co. Coors continued to make mortars and pestles, usually marked COORS, U.S.A.

A.85

THUEMLER MFG.
PITTSBURGH, PA.

This company's mark is found on advertising mugs, etc. of the early 1900s.

BRITISH ROYAL COAT OF ARMS MARKS

The British Royal Coat of Arms consists of a lion and a unicorn with a crown-topped shield between them. What Americans call the English or the British Coat of Arms is called the Royal Coat of Arms in Great Britain. Barber sometimes called it simply "the English mark." Whatever the name, it was frequently used as a mark both in this company and in Britain. It might appear strange that American companies would use this uniquely British mark. The reason was simple economics. The American public, for many reasons, preferred British or other imported wares. To compete, American companies resorted to deception. Copying the British Arms mark was an obvious way to achieve this deception. It is worth noting that the first commercially successful American company to make whiteware exclusively used only a very proper-looking Royal Arms mark. This was the Jersey City Pottery of Rouse and Turner. Barber pictured only the one British Royal Arms mark for this company from the 1850s to c.1880. More than 25 American companies used the British Arms mark, some using two or more versions. A few companies used a two-lions variant of the mark; others used whimsical or satirical simulations of the Royal Arms mark. Some continued to use the British Royal Coat of Arms to mark whiteware right into the twentieth century.

Another similar practice was using as marks the coats of arms of various American states. The coats of arms of New Jersey and Pennsylvania were most often used. Other included New York, Massachusetts, Maryland, and Michigan. See page 107.

The following several pages show the British Royal Coat of Arms marks used by American companies that did not include company names, initials or other distinguishing words as part of the mark. (If the Arms mark does have the company name, initials, or other distinguishing words, use the index to identify it.) Since some British companies also used the Royal Arms as marks without company names or initials, the lack of same does not necessarily indicate an American mark. However, all the Royal Arms marks used by British companies that I have seen have a central shield that is regular.* The first four marks on the following page have regular shields. American potters, on the other hand, frequently used the central shield to display company monograms or initials. Other left them blank. Included with the British Arms marks is a section titled the Two Lions Variant of the British Arms Mark. Also included is a page of American states coats of arms used as marks.

* There was at least one early English company that depicted pastoral scenes in the central shield; however, I've yet to see an English mark with company initials or a monogram inside the shield.

BRITISH COAT OF ARMS MARKS

See also page 99.

East End Pottery
See no.64 on p.28.

Wheeling Pottery Co.
See no.193 on p.77.

Steubenville Pottery Co.
See no.163 on p.67.

The first two marks are almost identical. The key difference is the *star* under the Wheeling mark. The crown atop the shield is slightly larger on the Wheeling mark. The Steubenville mark is different in three ways. First, it has a wide border around the shield. Second, there is an *S* and *C* under the shield. Since the mark may be quite small, these letters may be difficult to see. Finding them, however, would confirm the mark as that of the Steubenville Pottery. A third difference is that the horn on the unicorn is longer on the Steubenville mark.

Peoria Pottery Co.
See no.138 on p.59.

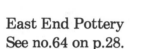

Akron China Co.
See no.2 on p.11.

American China Co.
See no.7 on p.12.

The Peoria mark is like the three marks above except that it has iron stone china, not royal ironstone china, above the shield. Note also that it has a wide border around the shield like the Steubenville mark. The Akron China and the American China marks are virtually identical. There is just a tiny difference between the crowns and a very tiny difference between the unicorns' manes. Note that the initials on the shields are the same.

Peoria Pottery Co.
See no.138 on p.59.

Peoria Pottery Co.
See no.138 on p.59.

Ott & Brewer
See no.133 on p.57.

The marks above are similar but easily distinguished. The Peoria Pottery marks are fairly unique in that they have shields with empty centers. Note the O.&B. monogram on the shield of the Ott & Brewer mark.

L.B. Beerbower & Co.
See no.18 on p.15.

N.Y. City Pottery
See no.127 on p.55.

Pioneer Pottery Co.
See no.144 on p.61.

The three marks above and the one below are dissimilar; but, like all the marks in this section, they are difficult to identify because there are no distinguishing words or initials above or below the marks. In each case the shield is the key. Note the L.B.B.&Co. on the first shield, the J.C. (monogram for James Carr) on the N.Y. City Pottery shield, and the P.P.Co. on the shield of the Pioneer Pottery mark. Finally, note the G.P.Co. monogram on the Glasgow Pottery mark's shield below.

Glasgow Pottery
See no.82 on p.34.

These marks were not included in Barber's 1904 book of American marks.

This mark is for the Burford Bros. Pottery Co. that operated in East Liverpool, Ohio, from 1879 to 1904.

Gates and Ormerod say the mark above is for the Burford Bros. Pottery Co. and/or the Standard Pottery Co., both of East Liverpool, Ohio.

This mark is for the Burford Bros. Pottery Co. that operated in East Liverpool, Ohio, from 1879 to 1904.

This mark is for the Dresden Pottery (Potters Cooperative) of East Liverpool, Ohio. It dates c.1890. The D.P.W. monogram is for the Dresden Pottery Works. See company no.63 for more about Dresden.

This mark is for the Potters Cooperative Co. (Dresden Pottery) of East Liverpool, Ohio. The P.C. monogram is for the Potters Cooperative. This mark may have T.P.C. Co. and/or DRESDEN as part of the mark. The mark would date c.1882 to c.1890.

This mark is for the Union Potteries Co. of East Liverpool, Ohio, and Pittsburgh, Pa. They operated from 1894 to 1904.

These marks were not included in Barber's 1904 book of American marks.

This mark is for the National China Co. Gates and Ormerod say it was used after 1911 when the company moved from East Liverpool, Ohio, to Salineville, Ohio.

This mark is for C.C. Thompson Pottery Co. of East Liverpool, Ohio. Gates and Ormerod date it c.1915. E.L.O. may be under the mark.

This mark is for the D.E. McNicol Pottery Co. of East Liverpool, Ohio. It dates c.1900. See p.49 for the same mark but with the company's initials.

J. Hart Brewer helped to start a new company in Trenton, N.J., c.1894 after the Ott & Brewer Co. ceased operations. By c.1900 the company was in Mr. Brewer's name. He died in December of that year. The mark above could be for his company.

Gates and Ormerod say this mark is for the Standard Pottery Co. of East Liverpool, Ohio. They date the mark 1886 to c.1910. Because of the S.C. Co. monogram, I am a bit dubious.

I believe this mark is for the William Brunt Pottery Co. dating before 1894. Based upon the style and decoration of the ware marked, it may date back to the 1880s when the company was called William Brunt, Son & Co. See p.17.

This mark is the quintessence of the American version of the British Royal Coat of Arms mark. It is not a direct copy of any British mark, yet it reflects the spirit of the Royal Arms mark. There are many similar versions. Gates and Ormerod show one mark identical to this one (except for details of the lion and unicorn) attributing it to the Wallace & Chetwynd Pottery Co. I believe this and similar versions were used by many early companies. This mark was found on a c.1870 or 1880 platter.

TWO-LIONS COATS OF ARMS
(A Variant of the British Coat of Arms)

Anchor Pottery Co.
See no.12 on p.14.

Crown Pottery Co.
See no.57 on p.25.

Vodrey & Brother
See no.185 on p.74.

Except for the monogram in the central shield, these marks above are almost identical. The first monogram is A.P.; the second is C.P. Co.; the third is V. & B. (Bro.).

Vodrey & Brother
See no.185 on p.74.

Vodrey & Brother
See no.185 on p.74.

Steubenville Pottery Co.
See no.163 on p.67.

The first mark is like the three marks above except that the position of WARRANTED and IRON STONE CHINA has been reversed. Note the V.&B. (Bro.) monogram on shield. The next two marks are unique. Note the V. & BRO. on the shield of the middle mark. Note the S.P. Co. on the shield of the last mark. See p.104 for one more Two-Lions mark.

STATE COAT OF ARMS MARKS

New Jersey Coat of Arms

This mark is for the Trenton Pottery Works. See 177 on p.71.

A similar mark, including company initials, was used by several other companies. See nos. 69, 73, 85.

The Crescent Pottery used this mark with just IRON STONE CHINA under the mark. See 55 on p.24.

Maryland Coat of Arms

This mark was used only by the Maryland Pottery Co. See 109 on p.47.

Pennsylvania Coat of Arms
See nos. 19, 44, 110.

New York Coat of Arms

This mark was used only by the Onondaga Pottery Co. See 132 on p.57.

Massachusetts Coat of Arms

This mark was used only by the New England Pottery Co. See 123 on p.54.

HARD TO IDENTIFY AMERICAN MARKS

See 21.,
page 15.

E.B.P. Co.
(monogram)

See 21.,
page 16.

See 28.,
page 17.

See 42.,
page 22.

See 57.,
page 25.

This crown mark was used on dinner-ware. The crown must look *exactly* like this. There will be other crown marks with no words. Crowns are common on English and other world marks.

See 60.,
page 26.

See 68.,
page 30.

See 72.,
page 31.

See 90.,
page 37.

See 104.,
page 45.

HC

See 104.,
page 45.

M
CHINA
L

See 108.,
page 46.

See 109.,
page 47.

The letter A. before some of the numbers below indicates that mark as being in the Appendix.

See 31.,
page 19.

See 90.,
page 37.

See 102.,
page 41.

STONE CHINA
WARRANTED

See 109.,
page 47.

See 113.,
page 50.

See 118.,
page 52.

See 121.,
page 53.

CHINA

See 169.,
page 68.

See 172.,
page 70.

(incised)
See A.7.,
page 82.

See A.30.,
page 87.

See A.43.,
page 90.

See A.61.,
page 93.

See A.62.,
page 93.

This T.P.Co. monogram is in the center of a complex shield.

IRON STONE CHINA

See 114.,
page 51.

See 114.,
page 51.

See 119.,
page 53.

See 123.,
page 54.

See 123.,
page 54.

See 123.,
page 54.

See 123.,
page 54.

See 125.,
page 55.

See 125.,
page 55.

See 127.,
page 56.

See 196.,
page 79.

(with or without circle)
See 138.,
page 59.

See 130.,
page 56.

See 133.,
page 58.

See 140.,
page 60.

See 141.,
page 60.

See 185.,
page 75.

See 193.,
page 77.

See 193.,
page 78.

BANNER MARKS

These marks and dates are from *The East Liverpool, Ohio, Pottery District* by William Gates and Dana Ormerod. See *Historical Archaeology* Volume 16, Numbers 1 & 2, (1982).

c.1910

D.E. McNicol Pottery

1899-c.1901

McNicol-Smith Co.

1900-1907

McNicol-Smith Co.

c.1905

Cartwright Bros.

1900-1907

McNicol-Smith Co.

1900-1907

McNicol-Smith Co.

1885-1895

Dresden Pottery

1879-1890

Harker Pottery

c.1900

Dresden Pottery

c.1905

Cartwright Bros. Co.

A SELECTION OF DIFFICULT BRITISH MARKS

THE FOLLOWING BRITISH MARKS, IF USED ALONE, WOULD BE DIFFICULT TO IDENTIFY. REMEMBER, THESE ARE BRITISH, NOT AMERICAN, MARKS.

PRINCE OF WALES' CREST: ICH DIEN may be on a ribbon under the crest. This mark was also used by the Cook Pottery Co. of the United States; however, they used Etruria instead of Ich Dien.

A lion rampant (common on British marks)

Caduceus mark on the left.

The dove mark below is found with or without TRADE MARK.

(Monogram)

The above monogram is to be found on several British marks.

DERBY CROWN MARK 1878-1890 A D or Derby under crown on various earlier marks.

WORCESTER MARK (Later a crown is placed above for ROYAL WORCESTER MARK.) Notice the 51 in center.

BIBLIOGRAPHY

Altman, Seymour and Violet. *The Book of Buffalo Pottery*. Crown Publishers, New York. 1969.

Barber, Edwin AtLee. *The Pottery and Porcelain of the United States*. G.P. Putnam's Sons, New York. Three ed's. 1893, 1901, 1909.

Barber, Edwin AtLee. *Marks of American Potters*. Patterson and White Co., Philadelphia, 1904.

Beers, J.H. *The History of Armstrong County, Pennsylvania: Her People Past and Present*. J.H. Beers & Co., Philadelphia. 1914.

Cox, Warren E. *The Book of Pottery and Porcelain*. Crown Publishers, New York. 1944.

Cunningham, Jo. *The Collector's Encyclopedia of American Dinnerware*. Collectors Books, Paducah, Ky. 1982.

Evans, Paul. *Art Pottery of the United States*. Charles Scribner's Sons, New York. 1974.

Gates, William C., Jr. and Ormerod, Dana E. *The East Liverpool, Ohio, Pottery District: Identification of Manufacturers and Marks*. Published as Volume 16. Numbers 1-2 of the *Journal of the Society for Historical Archaeology*. 1982.*

Godden, Geoffrey. *Encyclopedia of British Pottery and Porcelain Marks*. Crown Publishers, New York. 1964.

Hammond, Dorothy. *Confusing Collectibles*. Wallace-Homestead Book Co., Des Moines, Ia. Second printing 1972.

Lehner, Lois. *Complete Book of American Kitchen and Dinner Wares*. Wallace-Homestead Book Co., Des Moines, Ia. 1980.

McCord, William B. *History of Columbiana County*. Biographical Publishing Co., Chicago. 1905.

McKee, Floyd W. *The Second Oldest Profession: A Century of American Dinnerware Manufacture*. Privately printed. 1966.

Ramsay, John. *American Potters and Pottery*. Tudor Publishing Co., New York. 1947.

Spargo, John. *Early American Pottery and China*. Garden City Publishing Co., New York. 1926.

Stout, Wilbur. *History of the Clay Industry in Ohio*. Published in the *Geological Survey of Ohio*, Series 4, Bulletin, 26, Columbus, Ohio. 1923.

Thorn, C. Jordan. *Handbook of Old Pottery and Porcelain Marks*. Tudor Publishing Co., New York. 1947.

*Society of Historical Archaeology, P.O. Box 231033, Pleasant Hill, CA 94523-1033.

INDEX

This index was carefully designed to make possible the easy identification of early American whiteware and porcelain marks. Pages 1-3 include a step-by-step procedure that will help you to use the index more efficiently. The term LATE U.S. means it was used after 1930. The index includes many British initials. These initials were usually part of a complex mark. British initials used on 19th century marks are often in fancy, difficult-to-read script. Initials used on early American marks are seldom difficult to read. The numbers given after the marks are page numbers, not company numbers. The letter A indicates the mark is found in the Appendix.

117

Alox — late U.S.

Alpha — see 24.

Alpine China — see 17.

Aluminia — Denmark

A.M. above an L. — England

Amazon Shape — see 48.

Amberg — Germany

American Beauty, An — see 45.

American China — see 12.

American China Co. — see 12., 97 (A.79)

American Chinaware Corp. — U.S. (c.1930)

American Fine China — U.S. (1960s)

American Girl — see 65.

American Heritage (Dinnerware) — late U.S.

American Limoges — U.S. (Limoges China Co. — 1930s+)

American Pottery (Co.) — see 38.

American Pottery Co. (Peoria, Ill.) — see 59.

Amstel — Holland

An American Beauty — see 45.

Most anchors are for various, often early, European marks.

Anchor (Pottery) — see 14.

an anchor — see 14., 46., 81 (A.3), 82 (A.6)

an anchor and castle (impressed) — England

an anchor and U.S. flag behind a banner — see 73.

Angdus, The (or Angelus) — see 89 (A.38)

two animals (winged) — see 35.

Annaburg — Germany

Annecy — France

A.P. with an anchor — see 81 (A.3)

A.P. monogram — see 14.

A.P. Co. (L.) — England

A.P.M. Co. — see 12.

Apollo — see 74.

Apsley, Pellatt & Co. — Eng. retailer

A.Q.W. Co. — see 11.

A.-R. — see 67.

Arcadia (China) — England

Arequipa — early U.S. art pottery

Arita — U.S. (1970s+)

Ardmore — see 51.

an armor-clad head — see 76.

Arms (Seal) of Maryland — see 47.

Arms (Seal) of Mass. — see 54.

Arms of Michigan — see 16.

Arms of N.J. — see 24., 30., 31., 36., 71

Arms of N.Y. — see 57.

Arms of Pa. — see 15., 22., 48.

Arno — see 79.

Most arrow marks are European.

an arrow — see 26., 37., 59., 98 (A.84)

Art; Sebring, Ohio — U.S. (1920s)

Artistic — see 18.

an artist's palette — see 14., 45.

an artists palette with S in center — U.S. (1940s+)

Art Pottery Co. — England

Art Wells Glazes — U.S. (Homer Laughlin - 1930s)

Arundel — see 22.

Asbury — England

Ashby — England

Ashworth — England

Atkinson & Co. — England (very early)

Atlas China — see 14.

Atlas China above a globe — England

Atlas China under a globe — late U.S.

Atona (really Latona) — see 69.

Ato (really Cato) Patterns — see 48.

Ault — England

Aurora China — see 78., 79.

Auxerre — France

Avalon — see 20., 22.

Avalon China — see 22.

Beech & Hancock — England

a beehive — see 78.

other beehives — England, etc.

plain beehive mark — Austria

Beerbower (,L.B.) & Co. — see 15.

two bees below a hive (B.xB. above) — see 78.

a beetle (scarab) — see 55.

Belfield & Co. — Eng. (Scotland)

a bell — see 13., 23.

a bell with J.B. or a bell in a wreath — Eng. (Scotland)

two bells (one almost hidden) — England

Bell China — see 15.

Bell Pottery Co., The — see 15.

Belle — see 66.

Belleek — see 23., 42., 45., 58., 79., 83 (A.11)

Belleek and Co. Fermanagh — famous Irish Belleek

Belleek under hound & harp — famous Irish Belleek

Belle Vue (Pottery) — England

Bellview — see 64.

Bellvue — France (English-style whiteware)

Belmar — see 64.

Belva China — see 69.

Benedikt — Germany

Bennett, B. & W. — see 15.

Bennett, E. — see 16.

Bennett's — see 15.

Bennett, William — England

Bennington — see 73.

Bentley — England

Berkeley — see 34.

Berkeley on a clover — late U.S.

Berlin — see 14., 42., 64.

Berlin (really Oberlin) — see 42.

Beula (on map of Ohio) — see 66.

Bevington & Co. — Eng. (Wales)

B.F.B. (or & B.) — England

B.F.(K.) — Belgium

B.G. — England

B.G. & W. — England

B.G.P. Co. — England

Biltmore — see 12.

Bilton(s) — England

Bing & Grondahl — Denmark

a bird (dove?) holding a scroll or ribbon — see 24.

a bird on/above a globe — see 22.

a bird (Phoenix) above a crown — see 15., 85 (A.16)

a bird's head holding an S. — see 72.

Birks (various) — England

Bishop (& Stonier) — England

a bison (buffalo) — see 18., 41., 42.

Blackhurst — England

Blair — U.S. (1940s and 1950s)

Blair, A.C., China Studios — U.S. (1940s+)

Blairs China — England

Block — U.S. (1930s+)

Bloor (W.) — see 16.

other Bloor — England

Blue John (Pottery) — England

Blue Willow (by Royal) — U.S. (1950s)

B. - M. — see 19.

B.M. & Co. — see 19.

B.M. & Co. over Saracen Pottery — Eng. (Scotland)

B.M. & T. under a swan — England

Boch — Luxemburg or Germany

Boch Freres — Belgium

Bodley — England

Bonita — see 75.

Bonn (Royal) — Germany

Boote (,T. & R.) — England

Booth (various) — England

Bordeaux — see 51.

other Bordeaux — France

Borgano — Italy

Boston-1854 (in oval or garter) — see 54.

Bott & Co. — England

Boutet — France

Bovey — England

a bow and arrow — see 37.

Bowers, G.F. — England

Bowman, George H. — see 23.

Boyle — England

B.P. Co. — see 15., 17., 104.

also B.P. Co. (Ltd.) — England

B.P.M. — Germany

Bradley (various) — England

Brameld — England

Brannam, C.H. — England

Brentleigh Ware — England

Bretby — England

Brevete — France

Bridgwood (& Son) — England

Brighton Pottery — see 16.

Bristol — see 31.

other Bristol — England

Britannia (Pottery) — England

British (Royal) Coat of Arms — see pp.99 to 105.

British Coat of Arms marks with Stone China and a number under the Arms are English marks.

Brock — late U.S.

Brooklyn — see 20.

Brough & Blackhurst — England

Brown, Paisley — Eng. (Scotland)

Brown's Pottery — U.S. (1920s+)

other Brown — England

Brownfield (& Son or Sons) — England

Brownhills — England

Brub(d)ensul — see 16.

Brunt Art Ware — see 18.

Brunt (used alone) — England

Brusché — late U.S.

Brush (Ware) — U.S. (late 1920s+)

Brush-McCoy — see 18.

B.S. & T. — England

B.T.P. Co. — England

Buckley, Wood & Co. — England

a buffalo — see 18., 41., 42.

Buffalo China — see 18.

Buffalo Pottery — see 18.

a bug (scarab beetle) — see 55.

Bunting, W.C. — U.S. (1940s+)

Buntingware — U.S. (1970s+)

Burford (Bros.) — see 18., 19.

Burford's (China or Porcelain) — see 19.

Burgess (various) — England

Burgess & Campbell — see 38.

Burgess & Co. — see 38.

Burgess & Mountford — see 82. (A.5)

Burleigh Ware — England

Burlington (Ware) — England

Burslem — Eng. (Staffordshire)

B.W. — U.S. (Bailey-Walker 1920s)

B.W. & B. — England

B.W. & Co. — England

B. - W. (over an M.) — England

B.W.M. (& Co.) — England

121

a C. over N.A. — England
C. & B. — England
C. & Co. — England
C. & D. — England
C. & E. (Ltd.) — England
C. & F. — Eng. (Scotland)
C. & F. (really G. & F.) — see 88. (A.34)
C. & G. — England
C. & H. — England
C. & M. — England
C. & P. Co. under Denver — see 26.
C. & R. — England
C. & W. — England
C. & W.K.H. (with palm tree) — England
C.A. (over an L.) — England
C.A. & Co. (Ltd.) — England
C.A. & Sons — England
Caen — France
Caldas — Portugal
California — see 27., 43.
Cambridge — see 19.
Cameo Ware — U.S. (1940s)
Campbell — see 38.
Campbellfield — Eng. (Scotland)
Camwood Ivory — late U.S.
Candle Light (with Limoges) — U.S. (1940s)
Candy Ware — England
Canonsburg China — see 20.
Canonsburg Pottery — mostly late U.S., see 20.
Canton China — see 67.
C.A.P. monogram — see 19.
Capitol Ivory — see 69.
Cardigan — Eng. (Wales)
Careys — England
Caribe (China) — U.S. (1950s+)

Carlsbad — Austria (Bohemia), now Czech.
Carlton Ware — England
Carnation — see 73.
Carnation with McNicol — see 49.
Carr & Clarke — see 38.
Carr China — see 20.
Carr, James — see 56.
Carr, J. (& Sons) — England
Carrig(aline) — Ireland
Carrollton China — see 20.
Carrollton Pottery Co. — see 20.
Carter — England
Cartwright Bro's. — see 20., 21.
Casino (by Limoges) — U.S. (c.1950)
Castleton (China) — U.S. (1940s+)
a cat (panther or tiger) head — see 31.
a cat and a goose (swan) — see 28.
Cat Tail — late U.S.
Catalina (Island) — U.S. (1930s+)
Cato Pattern — see 48.
Cauldon — England
C.B. (over an F.) — England
C.B. (over an L.) — England
C.B. over a number — England
C.B. (P.) Co. — see 21.
C. Bro's. Co. — see 21.
C.C. Co. (initials or monogram) — see 25.
C.C.T. — see 81. (A.4)
C.C. Thompson & Co. — see 94. (A. 64)
C.C.T.P. Co. — see 69., 70.
C.C.T.P. Co. monogram — see 93. (A.61)
C.D.M. — French Limoges
C.E. & M. — England
Century Service Corp. — late U.S.
Ceramic Art Co. — see 45.
Cetem Ware — England

Compton — England

Contemporary China Inc. — U.S. (1960s)

Continental Kilns — U.S. (1940s+)

Conway — England

Cook & Hancock — see 24.

Cook Pottery Co. — see 23., 84 (A.15)

Cooke & Hulse — England

Cooper — England

Coors — see 23.

Coors, H.F. — late U.S.

Copeland — England

Copeland-Spode — England

Coral (Shape) — see 18.

Coral-Craft — U.S. (1940s)

Cordey China — late U.S. (porcelain)

Coreopsis — see 22.

Corinne — see 73.

Cork & Edge — England

Corn, W.E. — England

Cornell — see 42., 113.

Corns China Co. — see 50.

Corona — England

Cotton, Elijah — England

Cowan — U.S. art pottery (W.W.I to 1931)

Coxon & Co. — see 24.

Coxon Belleek — see 24.

C.P. Co. — see 22., 25., 85 (A.19)

C.P. Co. under a globe — see 22.

C.P. Co. under a U.S. Shield — see 22.

C.P. Co. Ltd. — see 22.

also C.P. Co. (Ltd.) — Eng. (Scotland); has a thistle on mark

Craftsman Dinnerware — U.S. (1930s+)

Creil — France

Cremorne (Opaque Porcelain) — see 47.

Crescent (Pottery) — see 24.

Crescent China — see 24.

a crescent — look under moon

Crocker — England

Cronin (China) — U.S. (1930s+)

Crooksville (China Co.) — see 24., 25., 86 (A.22-28), 98 (A.82)

a cross (Maltese type) — see 38., 58.

crossed swords, etc. — common German Meissen mark; used by many other European countries.

Crown marks are very common European marks. Crowns are often a part of English marks. Crowns with initials below were common early European marks. The marks below are American.

a crown — see 13., 19., 25., 38., 92 (A.55)

a crown (no words) — see 25.

a crown above a circle — see 31., 34., 43., 46., 78.

a crown above a circle (fleur-de-lis in center) — see 78.

a crown above a globe — see 35.

a crown above a G.C.M. & Co. monogram — see 53.

a crown above an R in circle — see 31.

a crown above REX. — see 25.

a crown above a shield — see 51.

a crown in a circle — see 28., 38., 70.

a crown in an oval — see 47.

a crown in a wreath — see 16.

a crown (N.E.P. monogram in center) — see 54.

a crown (Royal Crown, Etruria) — see 58.

a crown (a sword behind crown) —
    see 58.

a crown with an E in center — see 54.

a crown with a dragon on tóp — see 75.

a crown with a Phoenix Bird on top
    — see 15.

Crown — see 25.

Crown Brand — late U.S.

Crown Chelsea — England

Crown (Dresden) Ware — England

Crown Ducal — England

Crown Hotel Ware — see 25.

Crown Ovenware — U.S. (1930s+)

Crown Porcelain — see 25.

Crown Potteries Co. — late U.S.,
    — see 25.

Crown Pottery (on circle) — England

Crownford Ware — England

C.S. above an A. on a shield —
    Germany

C.T. (under eagle) — Germany
    (porcelain)

C.T.M. (& Sons) — England

Cuban — see 76.

Cube — England (teapots)

Cumbow China — U.S. (1930s+)

Cunningham & Pickett — late U.S.
    — see 95.

Cunningham Industries, Inc. —
    late U.S.

Cupid — see 32.

C.W. (as initials or monogram) — Eng.

D. & C. over an L. — England

D. & Co. — French Limoges

D. & D. — see 62., 63., 94 (A.69)

D. - D. — see 62., 63.

Dagoty — France (porcelain)

Dainty — see 24.

Dakota — see 42.

Dale & Davis (under British
    Arms) — see 62., 63.

Dal(l)witz — Austria, now Czech.

Daniel (& Sons) — England

Daniell — England (retailer)

Darte Freres — France

Davenport — England

Davis, I. (under British Arms) —
    see 62., 63.

Davis, I. (under shield) — see 62., 63.

Davis, J.H. — England

Dawson — England

Day (on artist's palette) — see 66.

Daybreak — see 48.

D.B. & Co. — England

D.C. — England

D. - D. — see 62., 63.

Deakin (& Son) — England

Dean, Jesse — see 68.

other Dean — England

Deck — France

Decoration — see 48.

Decoro Pottery — England

Dedham Pottery — see 26.

a deer (stag) head in circle — see 75.

two deer standing (in circle) —
    see 16.

Defender — see 19.

Delaware Pottery — see 26.

Delft D.C. — see 23., 84 (A.12)

Delphine (China) — England

D.E. McNicol — see 49.

D.E. Mc.N.P. Co., (The) — see 49.,
    90 (A.43)

DeMorgan — England (art pottery)

DeMoustiers — France

Denaura — see 26.

Denby — England

Denver — see 26., 33.

Denver C. & P. Co. — see 26.

Depose — French Limoges

Derby — see 31.

other Derby — England

Derry China Co. (on shield) — see 26.

DeSoto China — see 62.

Detroit — see 42.

Detroit over K.T.K. — U.S. (1920s)
   — see 43.

Devon — England

Dewey — see 28.

D.F.H. (Co.) monogram — see 22.

D.F.H. (or Hayes) & Co. — see 47.

Diamond — see 38.

Diamond (China) — see 16., 90 (A.46)

a diamond — see 16., 39., 48., 54.,
   90 (A.46)

a diamond (baseball?) — see 55.

a diamond with circle inside — see 16., 48.

a diamond (with H inside) — see 20., 37.

a diamond (with M inside) — see 33.

a diamond (with W inside) — see 78.

a diamond (with warranted fireproof)
   — see 60.

Diana — see 48.

Dicker Ware — England

Dillon — England

Dillwyn (& Co.) — Eng. (Wales)

Dixie — see 85 (A.19)

D.L. & Co. (or & Son, or & S.) —
   Eng. (Scotland)

D. M. & S. — Eng. (Scotland)

Doccia — Italy

Doctor Syntax — Eng. (Clews)

Don — see 66.

Don, Edward, Co. — U.S. (1940s+)

Don Pottery — England

Doric (China) — England

Doris — see 48.

Doulton (Royal) — England

a dove holding a ribbon (Scroll) — see 24.

D.P. Co. (Ltd.) — England

D.P.W. monogram — see 27.

D.R. — see 29.

a dragon — see 81 (A.4), 88 (A.33)

a dragon — see griffin possibly

a dragon atop a crown — see 75.

a dragon-like figure (over CHINA)
   — see 57.

a dragon holding a ball — see 57.

two dragons holding shield — see 35.

Dresden — see 27., 28.

Drexel — see 70.

Dryden — U.S. (1940s+)

Ducal (Crown) — England

Duchess — see 79.

Dudson (Bros.) — England

Duesbury — England

Dumonte Fabrique — France

Dunmore — Eng. (Scotland)

Duqesne — see 48.

Durham China — England

an E. (really N.E.P. monogram) on a
   crown — see 54.

E. & B. (L.) — England

E. & C.C. — England

E. & G.P. — England

E. & H. — England

an eagle — see 29., 35., 41., 45.

Electric — see p. 18 (nos. 28., 31.)

Elkin (Knight) & Co. — England

Elkton — see 84 (A.14)

E.L.O. (for East Liverpool, Ohio)
common on U.S. marks; can't use to
identify mark

ELPCO — see 74.

Elsmere — see 20.

Elsmore & Forster (or & Son) — England

E.M. & Co. — England

Emery — England

E.M.K. over C. Co. — see 39.

Empire China — see 83 (A.10)

Empire (Pottery) — see 30.

Empire Ware or Works — England

Emundu — England

English Coat of Arms — see pp. 99 to 105

Enterprise Pottery Co. — see 30.

Epicure Cook Ware — late U.S.

E.P.P. Co. (initials or monogram)
— see 30., 87 (A.30)

Era (Ware) — England

E.S. Prussia — Germany

E.S. Suhl — Germany

Este — Italy

Esther — see 91 (A.53)

Eton — see 48.

E.T.P. Co. — see 30.

Etruria — see 23., 57., 58.

Etruria; Mellor & Co. — see 23.,
84 (A.13, A.14)

Etruria (Pottery Co.) — see 58.

Etruscan (not majolica) — see 47.

Etruscan Ivory — see 60.

Etruscan Majolica — see 60.

Eugenia — see 12.

Eureka — see 87 (A.31)

Evans (& Co.) — Eng. (Wales)

an F. under a crown — Germany
(porcelain)

F. & C. — England

F. & Co. — England

F. & H. — England

F. & R. — England

F. & R.P. (& Co.) — England

F. & S. (or & Sons) — England

F. & T. Co. — see 31.

Facon Porcelaine — France

Faenza — Italy

Falcon Ware — England

Fancy — see 43.

F.B. & Co. (over an F.) — England
— see 97 (A.80)

F.C. (& Co.) — England

F.C. Co. — see 32.

F.C. Co. monogram — see 31.

F.D. — England

three feathers with Etruria —
see 23., 83 (A.11)

three feathers with La Franchaise
— see 32.

Fell (& Co.) — England

Felspar (China or Porcelain) — England

Fenix — see 65.

Fenton (Works) — see 73.

other Fenton — England

Feraud — France

Ferrybridge — England

Festoon — see 34.

Fielding — England

Fiesta — U.S. (Homer Laughlin —
1930s+)

Gem Shape — see 74.

Geneva — see 64.

Genoa — see 48.

George, W.S. — see 33.

George H. Bowman Co. — see 23.

George Morley (& Son) — see 52.

George Tunnicliffe — see 68.,
   93 (A.60)

Geo. S. Harker & Co. — see 37.

Georgian Dinnerware — U.S. (1930s+)

G.F.B. (B.T.) — England

G.F.S. (Co.) — England

G.G. & Co. — England

G.G.W. — England

G.H. & Co. — England

G.H.B. Co. — see 23.

Gibson (& Sons) — England

Gien — France

Giesshubel — Germany

Ginder, S., & Co. — England

Ginori — Italy

G.J. as a monogram — England

G.L.A. & Bros. — England

Gladding, McBean & Co. — late U.S.

Gladstone — England

Glasgow China or Pottery — see 33., 34.

other Glasgow on mark — Eng. (Scotland)

G.L.B. & Co. — England

Glebe Pottery — England

Glendora — see 113.

Glen Rose — see 22.

Glenwood — see 93 (A.63)

Globe (Pottery or China) — see 34., 35.

other Globe Pottery — England

a globe — see 27., 34., 35., 51.

a globe (half submerged-U.S. flag on
   top) — see 67.

a globe held by lion & unicorn (an
   eagle on top) — see 24.

a globe in a circle — see 15., 57.

a globe in a square — see 19.

a globe in a wreath — see 19.

a globe pierced by a sword — see 16.

a globe under a crown — see 35.

a globe with IDEAL BB on a ribbon
   — see 18.

a globe with a lion on top — see 80.

a globe with O. WARRANTED B. across
   — see 58.

a globe with eagle holding shield
   in front — see 77.

a globe with a bird on top — see 22.

a globe with WARRANTED across —
   see 27., 51., 58.

a globe with wings — see 35.

G.M. & Son — see 52.

G.M.B. — late U.S.

G.M.C. monogram — England

G.M.T. Co. — U.S. (1940s+)

Godwin (T. or Thos., or T. & B.) — Eng.

Godwin & Flentke — see 88 (A.34)

Gold Medal/St. Louis — see 58.

Golden — see 33.

Golden Gate — see 45.

Golden Glo — U.S. (1970s)

Goldscheider — late Eng., late U.S.

Goldscheider (Wien) — Austria

Gonder — U.S. (1940s+)

Goode — England (retailer)

Goodfellow — England

Goodwin — see 88 (A.33)

Goodwin (Bros.) — see 35.

Goodwin Pottery Co. — see 35., 87(A.32)

Goodwins & Harris — England

Hall (various) — England

Hallcraft — U.S. (1950s+)

Hampshire Pottery — see 36., 37.

Hancock (,S.,) (& Sons) — England

Hamilton — England

Hammersley & Co. — England

two hands shaking (clasped) — see 56.

also two clasped hands mark used in
England but with no words or
initials accompanying mark

Hanley — England

Harding (& Cockson) — England

Hardmuth — Germany or Austria

Harker, Geo. S., & Co. — see 37.

Harker, Taylor & Co. — see 37.

Harkerware — U.S. (1950s+)

Harlequin — U.S. (1940s+)

Harmony House — late U.S.

a harness — see 35.

Hartley (,Greene) — England

Harvard — see 42., 48.

Harvey — England

Harvey (,Holland & Green) — England

Harwood — England

Haviland (& Co.) — French Limoges

Hawley (various) — England

Haynes — see 22.

Haynes, D.F., & Co. — see 47.

H.B. under British Arms — England

H.C. (really H.L.C.) monogram
— see 45.

Heath — U.S. (1940s+)

also Heath (various) — England

Heathcote (China) — England

Heather Hall — late U.S.

Helen — see 25.

Hendrickson, W.H. — see 68.

Henri Deux (J.B. Owens) — see 59.

Herculaneum — England

Herend — Hungary

Heritance — late U.S. (Harker)

H.F. in a diamond — England

H.F. Coors — late U.S.

H.F.W. & Co. Ltd. — England

H.H. & G. Ltd. — England

H.H. & M. — England

Hiawatha — see 86 (A.21)

Hill Pottery — England

Hines Bros. — England

H.J. (initials or monogram) — England

H.J.C. (over an L.) — England

H.J.W. (over a B.) — England

H.L. monogram — see 45.

H.L.C. monogram — see 45.

H.M.J. (or & J.) — England

H.N. & A. — England

Hobson — see 25.

other Hobson — England

Hoffman — U.S. (1940s+)

Holden — England

Holdfast Baby Plate — see 50.

Holland (& Green) — England

Hollins — England

Hollinshead — England

Hollitsch — Hungary

Holmes & Son — England

Home Flowers Dec. — see 22.

Homer Laughlin — see 43., 44., 45.,
88., 89.

Honiton — see 19.

other Honiton — England

Honore — France

Hopewell China — U.S. (1920s+)

Hornberg — Germany

Iron Stone China is a term found frequently on early American (and English) marks. It can't be used to identify a mark. Most ware with Iron Stone (Ironstone) China dates before 1900.

Iroquois (China) — mostly late U.S., — see 38.

Ivory — various marks with descriptive adjective — see page 95.

Ivory — see 16.

Ivory Porcelain — see 13., 95 (A.72)

I.V.W. in a diamond — see 39.

I.W. & Co. — England

J. & B. (L.) — England

J. & Co. — England

J. & C.W. — England

J. & E.M. — see 47., 48.

J. & E. Mayer — see 47., 48.

J. & G. (over an L.) — England

J. & G.A. — England

J. & M.P.B. & Co. — Eng. (Scotland)

J. & P. — England

J. & R.G. — England

J. & T.B. — England

J. & T.E. — England

J. & W.R. — England

Jackson (& Gosling) — England

Jackson, Royal — U.S. (1940s+)

Jackson (Vitrified) China — mostly late U.S.

Jacobi Adler & Co. — Germany

Jade Ware — see 13.

James Carr — see 56.

James L. Howard (around circle) — see 55.

Japonica — see 38.

J.B. — England and Scotland

J.B. under a swan — England

J.B. & Co. — England

J.B. & S. (or Son) — England

J.B.W. — England

J.C. — England

J.C. (as initials or monogram) — see 55., 56.

J.C. between two shields — see 81 (A.2)

J.C. over an L. — England

J. Co. (,J.E.) monogram — see 60.

J.D. & Co. — England

J.E. (& Co., or & S.) — England

J.E.J. — England

J.E.J. Co. (monogram) — see 60.

J.E.N. — see 14.

Jersey City (,N.J.) — see 38.

Jesse Dean — see 68.

Jewel — see 25.

J.F. & Co. — England

J.F.A. — England

J.F.E. Co. Ltd. — England

J.F. Steele — see 93 (A.59)

J.F.W. — England

J.G.S. & Co. — England

J.H. & Co. — England

J.H. Baum — see 14.

J.H.C. & Co. — England

Jiffy Ware — U.S. (1930s+)

J.J. & Co. — England

J.K. (L.) — England

J.M. (above an F.) — England

J.M. monogram — see 33.

J.M. & Co. — see 33., 34.

also J.M. & Co. — England and Scotland

J.M. & L. — England

J.M. & S. (or Son) — England

J.M. & S. Co. — see 34.

J.M. Co. — Eng. (Scotland)

John Maddock & Sons — see 47.

also John Maddock & Sons — England
(marked England)

John Moses — see 33.

Johnson (Bros.)   This English
company's marks are very common
in the U.S.

Johnson's (E. Liverpool) — U.S.
(1930s+)

Jones (various) — England

Jordan (Ware) — England

J.P. over an L. — French Limoges

J.P. & Co. — England

J.R. (& Co.) — England

J.R. (& F.C.) — England

J.R.B. & Co. — England

J.R.H. — England

J.S. & Co. — England

J.S.H. — England

J.S.S.B. — England

J.S.T. & Co. — see 37.

J.S.W. (initials or monogram) —
England

J.T. — England

J.T. & Co. — Eng. (Scotland)

J.T. (& S.) — England

J.T.H. — England

Juno — see 48.

J.V. (& S.) — England

J.W. & S. (or & Co.) — England

J.W. & Son — see 79., 80.

J.W.P. (& Co.) — England

J.W.R. — England

J.Y. — England

a K. on a "plain" crown — U.S. (1940s+)

a K. with Knowles — late U.S.

K. & B. — England

K. & Co. (B.) — England

K. & E. — England

K. & G. — France

K. & S. — see 43.

Karlsbad — Czech. (Bohemia), was
Austria

Kass (China) — U.S. (1930s+)

K.E. & B. — England

K.E. & Co. — England

K.E.B. — England

Keeling (various) — England

Kelsboro (Ware) — England

Kennedy (various) — England

Kenneth — see 32.

Kent, J. (or James) — England

Kenwood — late U.S.

Kettlesprings (Kilns) — U.S. (1950s+)

Keystone — see 75.

a keystone — see 22., 39., 75.

a keystone (with C.P. Co. Ltd.) — see 22.

a keystone in a wreath — see 39.

a keystone with word KEYSTONE in
center — see 75.

Keystone China (Co.) — late U.S.,
— see 39.

Kirkham — England

Kirkland — England

Klentsch — Germany

Klum — Germany

Knapper & Blackhurst — England

Knesl — Austria

Knight — England

a knight's head — see 76.

Knowles under a K. — late U.S.

Knowles, Edwin M. — see 39., 40.,
95 (A.71)

Knowles, Taylor & Knowles — see 41.,
42., 43.

Koenige Porzellan Manufactur —
Germany

Kokus (Stone) China — see 13.

Kosmo — see 65.

K.P.M. — Germany

K.S.P. — England

K.S.St.F. — Germany

K.T. & K. — see 41., 42., 43.

K.T. & Я. (reversed K.-monogram)
— see 42.

K.T. & K. under Detroit — U.S. (1920s)
— see 43.

an L. — see 45.

an L. (with oval through top) — see 55.

an L. in a circle (artist's palette on top)
— see 45.

an L. in a wreath — see 45.

L. & A. — England

L. & H. — England

L. & L. — England

L. & S. in a circle — see 55.

L. & Sons (Ltd.) — England

La Belle China — see 78.

L.A. Potteries — U.S. (1940s+)

Lafayette Porcelain under a wreath
— see 30.

La Francaise (Porcelain) — see 32.

Lakin — England

Lamberton (China) — see 46., 89 (A.39)

Lamberton (Scammell) China — see 89
(A.39)

Lamberton (Sterling) — see 89 (A.39)

Lambeth — England

Lancaster — England

Lane End — England

Langenthal — Switzerland

Langley — England

La Solana Potteries — U.S. (1940s+)

Latona — see 69.

Laughlin Bros. — see 44.

Laughlin (China) — see 44., 45.

Laughlin, Homer — see 43., 44., 45.

L.B.B. & Co. — see 15.

L.B. Beerbower & Co. — see 15.

L.C. Co. with PURITAN — U.S.
(Limoges China Co.-c.1920+)

L.E. & S. — England

Lear — England

Lee — see 93 (A.62)

other Leeds — England

Lefton China — Japan

Leigh Potters, Inc. — U.S. (c.1930)

Leigh Ware — U.S. (c.1930)

Leighton (Pottery) — England

Leland — see 69., 113.

Leneige — U.S. (1930s+)

Lenox — see 45.

Le Pere — U.S. (1930s+)

Lettin — Germany

Leveille — France

Liberty — see 62.

Liberty Hall Ironstone — late U.S.

Liberty Hotel China — see 13.

Lifetime China — late U.S.

Lille — France

Limoges — usually a French mark;
however, some American marks
deceptively use the word Limoges.
They are listed here:

Murphy & Co. — see 53.

Mutual China Co. — mostly late, see 53.

M.V. & Co. — England

M.W. monogram — see 23.

M.W. & Co. — England

M.W. & H. — England

Myatt — England

Myott — England

M.Z. — Germany

Nantgarw — Eng. (Wales), porcelain

Naomi — see 113.

Napco — U.S. (late 1930s+)

Nasco — U.S. (1930s)

Nassau — see 51.

Nassau China Co. — see 98 (A.81)

Nast — France

National China (Co.) — see 53.

National Dinner-Ware — see 53.

Nautilus — see 35.

Nautilus Porcelain — Eng. (Scotland)

N.C. Co. — see 53.

N.C. Co. monogram — see 53.

N.C.P. Co. — see 54.

Neale (various) — England

Nelson Ware — England

N.E.P. monogram — see 54.

N.E.P. Co. — see 54.

Neuleininger — Germany

Neumark — Germany

New Bridge Pottery — England

New Castle China — see 54.

New Era — see 18.

New Hall — England

New Jersey Coat of Arms — see 24., 30., 31., 36., 71.

New Jersey Pottery Co. — see 54.

New Park — England

Newport — England

New York Coat of Arms — see 57.

New Wharf — England

N.G. (F.) — Germany

N.H. & Co. — England

Niderville — France

Nile — U.S. (c.1930)

Nile Shape — see 48.

ninety four (94) on a shield — see 17.

Nippon, Hand Painted — Japan before c.1920

N.J. Pottery Co. — see 54.

N.M.P. Co. — see 55.

Norcrest — very late (Japan)

Nordd Steingut — Germany

Noritake — Japan

Norton — see 73.

Noue (Nove) — Italy

Nove — Italy

Nowatny — Austria (Bohemia), now Czech.

N.S. (impressed) — England

N.W.P. Co. — England (New Wharf)

N.Y.C.P. (Pottery) — see 56., 81 (A.1)

Nymphenburg — Germany

O. & B. (initials or monogram) — see 57., 58.

O.-B. — see 58.

O. & B. Co. (initials and monogram) — see 58.

O. & Co. — see 26.

Oakwood — see 19.

Oakwood China — U.S. & foreign blanks (c.1915)

O.-B. — see 58.

P.B & Co. (or & H.) — England

P.B.(L.) — England

P.B. & S. — England

P. Bros. — England

P. Co. (actually I.P. Co.) — see 38.

P.C.P. Co. — see 59. (Paden City)

Peach-Blo — U.S. (Limoges China Co. — c.1930)

Pearce — England (retailers)

Pearl (China Co.) — U.S. (1930s+)

Pearl Ivory by Limoges — U.S. (c.1930)

Pearl Porcelain — see 82 (A.8)

Pearl White — see 35.

Pearson — England

Peasantware — U.S. (1930s)

Pecs — Hungary

Pefaro (really Pesaro) — Italy

Pellatt — England (retailers)

Pennova China — see 68.

Pennsbury Pottery — U.S. (1950s+)

Pennsylvania Coat of Arms — see 15., 22., 48.

Pennsylvania Pottery (or China) — see 78., 79.

Peoria, Ill. — see 59.

Perfect — see 113.

Perfection — see 104.

Perlee Inc. — U.S. (late 1920s)

Pesaro — Italy

Petroscan — see 56.

Pfaltzgraff — see 60.

P.G. in circle with Limoges — England

P.G. Co. — see 62. (Pope-Gosser)

P.H. & Co. — England

P.H. Co. — England

P.H.G. (or & G.) — England

Phillips (various) — England

Phillis — see 48.

a phoenix bird on crown — see 15., 85 (A.16)

Phoenix China (Ware) — England

Pick, Albert — see 60.

Pickard China — late U.S.

Pickard, Hand Painted — see 61.

Pickman (y. ca.) — Spain

Pierce & Co. — England

Pillivu(y)t — France

Pinder — England

Pink Willow (by Royal) — U.S. (1950s)

Pioneer Pottery Co. — see 90 (A.48)

Pioneer Pottery Works — see 61.

Pirkenhammer — Austria

Pisgah Forest — late U.S. art pottery

Plant — England

three plumes — see 23., 32., 83 (A.11)

Pluto — see 32.

Podmore — England

Pointon(s) — England

Poole — England

Poole & Stockton — see 68.

Pope & Lee — see 68.

Pope-Gosser — see 62.

Poppy — see 22.

Poppy Trail — late U.S.

Porcelier — late U.S., see 62.

Porc-Granite — see 67.

Portland — see 27.

Possil Pottery — Eng. (Scotland)

Potomac — see 48.

Potters Co-operative Co. (The) — see 26., 28.

Pottery Guild — U.S. (1930s & 1940s)

Poulson Brothers — England

Pountney & Co. (Ltd.) — England

Pouyat — French Limoges

Powell & Bishop — England

P.P. initials in a diamond — England

P.P. (Works) — see 61.

P.P. Co. (initials) — see 59., 61.

P.P. Co. (as various monograms) —
see 59., 61., 79.

P.P. Co. Ltd. — England

P.P. Coy L. — England

P.P. Works — see 61.

Prag — Czech.

Pratt (& Co.) — England

Price (Bros.) — England

Primavesi, F., (& Son) — Eng.
(Scotland)

Princess — see 66.

Princess (on a globe) — see 90 (A.44)

Princeton — see 42., 113.

Priscilla — see 34.

Progress — see 34.

Provincial Ware — see 86 (A.25)

P.S. above an L. — England

Psyche — see 34.

Puritan — see 76.

Puritan over L.C. Co. — U.S.
(Limoges China Co. — c.1920+)

Puriton (Slip Ware) — U.S. (c.1940 to
c.1960)

P.W. & Co. (or & W.) — England

Queen — see 33.

Quimper — France

Quincy — see 43.

an R. inside a circle (crown on top)
— see 31.

an R. above a C. — U.S. (1950s+)

R. & C. — England

R. & D. — England

R. & M. — England

R. & M. Co. — England (Rowland &
Marsellus)

R. & N. — England

R. & P. — England

R. & S. over an L. — England

R. & T. (under British Coat of Arms)
— see 39.

also R. & T. — England

R. & W. — England

a rabbit facing forward — see 22.

a rabbit (side view) — see 26.

Radford(s) or Radfordian — England

Raleigh — see 73.

Ratcliffe — England

Rathbone — Eng. (Scotland)

Ravenscourt — England

Ravenscroft — late U.S.

Ravenwood — see 91 (A.49)

R.B. & S. — England

R.C. monogram (Sebring, Ohio) — U.S.
(1930s+), see 63.

R.C. under a crown — Germany

R.C. & Co. — England and Scotland

R.E. & Co. — see 12.

Real Ivory (on a shield) — see 22.

a rectangle (with J.C., Stone Porcelain)
— see 56.

Red Wing — see 63.

Reed — England

Reeves, J. — England

Regal — see 35.

Regal (Fine China) — late U.S.

Regal Ware — England

Regina — see 25., 89 (A.41)

Reid(s) — England

Rena — see 25.

Revere under a wreath — see 30.

Revere, Paul, (Pottery) — see 63.

Revere China — see 11.

Rex — see 25.

R.G.S. (& Co.) — England

R.F. & S. — England

R.H. (& S.) — England (also Scotland)

R.H. & Co. — England

Rheinsberg — Germany

R.H.P. (& Co.) — England

two ribbons forming a circle — see 33.

two ribbons forming a near circle — see 31.

Ridgewood (Fine China) — U.S. (1970s)

Ridgways (various) — England

Rieti — see 54.

Riley(s) — England

Riviera — late U.S. (Homer Laughlin)

R.L. over an L. — French Limoges

R.M. (& S.) — England

R.M.W. & Co. — England

Robertson & Sons — see 22.

Robineau — see 67.

Robinson — England

Rochester — see 43.

Rochester Porcelain — see 78.

Rocket — see 18.

Rockingham (Works) — England

Rococo — see 57.

Rogers (& Son) — England

Roloc (McNicol) — late U.S.

Roma — Italy

Roma (yellow glaze) — U.S. (c.1930)

Rorstrand — Sweden

Rose, John, (& Co.) — England

Rosenthal — Germany

Roseville, (O. or Ohio) — late U.S.,
— see 63. (no. 150)

Roseville, U.S.A. — late U.S.
— see 63. (no. 152)

Rosina — England

Roslyn — England

Rowland & Marsellus — England

Royal — often used on English and
other European marks. It is also
to be found on American marks as
seen below.

Royal — see 25., 71., 74.

Royal Albert — England

Royal Albion — England

Royal Bayreuth — Germany

Royal Blue (China or Porcelain) —
see 38., 82 (A.5)

Royal Bonn — Germany

Royal Cauldon — England

Royal China — see 38., 63., 83 (A.9)

Royal (China, Inc.) — U.S. (1930s+),
— see 63.

by Royal (China) — U.S. (1940s+), see 63.

Royal (China), (Sebring, Ohio) — U.S.
(1930s+), see 63.

Royal Copenhagen — Denmark

Royal Copley — U.S. (1940s+)

Royal Crown — see 58.

Royal Crown Derby — England

Royal Doulton — England

Royal Dux — Czech. (Bohemia)

Royal Haeger — late U.S.

Royal Harvest — U.S. (1960s)

Royal Jackson — U.S. (1940s+)

Royal Lancastrian — England

Royal Porcelain — see 34., 46.

Royal Semi-Granite — see 71.

Schmider — Germany

Schmidt — Germany

Schoelcher — France (porcelain)

Schofield — England

Schuman(n) — Germany

Schutz(Marke) — Germany

S. Clement — France

Scotia Pottery — England

Scott (various) — England

S.E. — England

a sea serpent — see 75.

Sebring (Sebring's) — see 13.

Sebring Bros. & Co. — see 13.

by Sebring — late U.S., see 13.

Sebring, E.H., China Co. — see 64.

Sebring Porcelain, The — see 13.

Sebring Pottery Co. — see 13.

S.E.G. — see 63. (no.149)

Segovia — Spain

Selb — Germany

Semi Granite — see 24., 71.

Semi Porcelain (on ribbon) — see 62.

Semi Porc' Balt. — see 22.

Sept. 19, 1871 (Pat.) — see 55.

Sequoia Ware — late U.S.

a serpent, sea — see 75.

Severn — see 24.

Seville — Spain

Sevres — see 64.

Sevres is famous French porcelain;
   however, see number 158 (p.64) in this
   book for "American Sevres" marks
   first! These marks are rather
   common in this country.

Sewell (& Co.) — England

S.F. & Co. — England

S.H. (& S. or & Sons) — England

S.H. over a D. — England

Shaw (SH AW) — see 16.

other Shaw — England

Shawnee — U.S. (1930s to c.1960)

a shell (scallop or clam) — see 54.

Shelley — England

Shelton Ware — England

Shenandoah (is by Paden City) — late
   U.S., see 59.

Shenango China (Co.) — see 65.

Shenango Pottery Co. — see 65.

Shepherd, A., & Co. — England

a shield — see 18., 22., 23., 26., 27., 29

a shield (U.S.) — see 22., 27., 29., 33.,
   49., 56., 74.

a shield (draped) — see 49., 51., 63., 71.

a shield inside a wreath — see 52.

a shield (with Dainty, Melloria, Severn)
   — see 24.

a shield with M.W. monogram — see 23.

a shield with S.C.C., Akron — see 67.

a shield (with U.S.A. across) — see 29.

the U.S. Shield — see 22., 27., 29., 33., 49., 56., 74.

two shields (one U.S., one British) — see
   38., 51., 56., 80., 95., 96.

Shore & Coggins — England

Shorthose — England

Sigsbee — see 73.

Simpson(s) — England

Sirius — see 34.

S.J. (B. or Ltd.) — England

S.K. & Co. — England

S.M. Co. — see 62.

Smith (various) — England

Smith, Fife & Co. — see 65.

Smith-Phillips (China) — see 65., 66.,
   93 (A.58)

Stone China, Warranted — see 47.

St. Paul — see 42.

Stubbs — England

Sudlow (& Sons) — England

Suhl — Germany

Suisse — Switzerland

a sunburst (W in center) — see 55.

Sunray Pottery — England

Superior Hall Quality — U.S. (1930s+)

Sutherland China — England

Swansea — Eng. (Wales)

Swinnertons — England

swords (crossed) — see crossed swords

Sydney — see 69.

Sylvan China — England

Syracuse China — mostly late U.S.,
    see 57.

a T. in a star or a circle — see 70.

T. & B. — England

T. & B.G. — England

T. & C.F. — England

T. & K. — England

T. & K. (L. in the middle) — England

T. & L. — England

T. & R.B. — England

T. & T. — England

T. & V. — French Limoges

T.A. & S.G. — England

Tacoma — see 42., 51.

T.A. McNicol Pottery Co. — see 50.

Tams (,J.) — England

Tatler, W.H., Decorating Co. — see
    67., 68., 93 (A.60)

Taylor & Kent — England

Taylor, Lee & Smith Co. — see 68.

Taylor, Smith & Taylor — see 68., 69.

Taylorton — U.S. (1960s)

T.B. — England

T.B. & Co. — see 17.

also T.B. & Co. — England

T.B. & S. — England

T.B. & S.P. Co. — see 17.

T.B.G. — England

T.C. monogram — U.S. (1960s+)

T.C. over an L. — England

T.C.G. & Co. (Ltd.) — England

T.C.W. — England

Teco — mostly early U.S. art pottery

Teinitz — Austria, now Czech.

TEPECO — see 71.

Teplitz — Austria (Bohemia), now
    Czech.

Tetschen — Austria, now Czech.

Texas — see 20., 113.

T.F. — England

T.F. & Co. — England

T.F. & S. (Ltd.) — England

T.F. & Sons (monogram) with
    Cobridge — England

T.G. — England

T.G. & T.B. — England

T.G.B. — England

T.G.G. & Co. — England

T.H. & P. — England

Theodor Paetsch — Germany

Thomas on shield — Germany
    (porcelain)

Thomas China Co. — see 69.

Thompson — see 70., 93 (A.63)

Thompson with U.S.A. — U.S.
    (1930s), see 70.

also Thompson — England

Thompson, C.C., & Co. — see 94 (A.64)

Union (China) — see 73.

Union Porcelain Works — see 72.

United States Pottery Co. of
Bennington, Vermont — see 73.

United States Shield — see 22., 27.,
29., 33., 49., 56., 74.

Universal (Potteries) — U.S.
(1930s-1950s)

Universal Ware — England

Unwin, Holmes & Worthington —
England

U.P.C. monogram (letters intertwined)
— see 73.

U.P. Co. monogram — see 72.

Upchurch — England

Upper Hanley — England

U.P.W. above an eagle's head — see 72.

Ursula — see 113.

U.S. (on a shield) — see 74.

Usona — see 88 (A.33)

U.S.P. on a ribbon — see 73.

U.S. Pottery Co. (Wellsville, O.)
— see 73., 74.

U.S. Shield — see 22., 27., 29., 33.,
49., 56., 74.

Utah — see 42.

Utopia — see 24.

V. & B. (initials or monogram) — see 74.

V. & B. — Germany (Mettlach)

V. & Bro. (on shield held by two
lions) — see 74.

a vase — see 39., 40.

a vase in a triangle — see 58.

a vase with ribbons on sides — see 48.

Vaudrevange — Germany (Mettlach)

Vellum — U.S. (1930s+)

Venable — England

Vernon on a shield — see 23.

Vernon (Kilns) — late U.S.

Vernon Ware — late U.S.

Verona (China) — see 68., 97 (A.78)

Verus — see 57.

Vesta — see 66.

Victor — see 31.

Victoria — see 70.

Vigilant — see 19., 34.

Villeroy (& Boch) — Germany
(Mettlach)

Virginia — see 42.

Vistosa — see 69.

Vodrey & Bro. — see 74.

Vohann — U.S. (1950s+)

Volkmar — early U.S. art pottery

Volpato, G. — Italy

V.P. Co. — see 75.

a W. (as fancy monogram in a wreath)
— see 78.

a W. in a diamond — see 78.

a W. in a sunburst — see 55.

W. & A. — England

W. & B. (Ltd.) — England

W. & C. — see 75.

also W. & C. — England

W. & C. (P.) Co. — see 75.

W. & Co. over a B. — England

W. & E.C. — England

W. & J.B. — England

W. & J.H. — England

W. & L. — England

W. & S.E. — England

W. & Sons — England

W. & W. over a B. — England

W. & W. (really W.W.&) Co. —
England

W.A. & Co. — England

W.A. & S. — England

W.A.A. (& Co.) — England

Waco China — see 29.

WACO, Hand Painted — late U.S.

Wade (Heath) — England

Wagstaff & Brunt — England

Waldorf — see 51.

Walker (China), Bedford, Ohio — U.S.,
(late 1920s+)

other Walker — England

Wallace & Chetwynd — see 75.

Wallace & Co. — England

Wallace China — U.S. (1930s+)

Walley — England

Walrich — England

Walton — England

Warburton — England

Wardle — England

Warner-Keffer China Co. — see 65.

Warranted (around a globe) — see 15.

Warranted (in oval above crown)
— see 47.

Warranted (through an oval) — see 26.

Warranted, P. under a crown —
England

Warwick (China) — see 76.

Washington — see 42.

Watcombe — England

Watson — Eng. (Scotland)

Watt (Oven Ware) — late U.S.

W.B. over an H. — England

W.B. (& S. or Son) — England

W.B. Jr. & Co. — see 17 (no. 27),
85 (A.16)

W.B.P. Co. — see 17., 18.

W.B.S. & Co. — see 17., 85 (A.16)

W.C. & Co. — England

W.C. Bunting — U.S. (1940s+)

W.C. Co. — see 62., 76., 94 (A.65)

W.E. — England

W.E.C. — England

Wedgwood (various) — England

Wedgwood (really WedgWood), J.
(John) — England

Weil Ware — U.S. (1940s+)

Weller (Pottery) — see 76.

Wells (with peacock) — U.S. (Homer
Laughlin — 1930s)

Wellsville (China Co.) — see 62.

Wellsville China — see 62.

W.E.P. Co. — see 76.

Wessel (Imperial) — Germany

West End (Pottery Co.) — see 77.

Western Gem — see 53.

Western Stoneware Co. — see 77.

Westward Ho — late U.S.

Westwood by Limoges — U.S.
(1930s+)

Wetley China — England

W.F. & Co. — England

W.F. & R. — England

W.H. (& Co.) — England

W.H. (& S.) — England

a wheel — see 33.

Wheeling (Gold) China, Wheeling,
W. Va. — late U.S.

Wheeling Decorating — late U.S.

Wheeling Pottery Co., The —
see 77., 78.

Wheelock — see 94 (A.66)

W.H.G. — England

W.H. Hendrickson — see 68.

Whieldon Ware — England

W.H.L. over an H. — England

W.H. Tatler Decorating Co. — see
  67., 68., 93 (A.60)

Wick China Co. — see 78., 79.

Wien — Austria

Wild Rose — U.S. (1940s+)

Wileman, J.F. — England

Willets — see 79.

Wilkinson (,A.J.) — England

William Flenke — see 88 (A.34)

Williamson's — England

Wilson — England

Wilton — see 38.

Wilton Ware — England

Windsor — see 48.

Winfield (China) — late U.S.

Winkle, F., & Co. — England

Winona — see 74.

Winterton — England

Witteburg — Germany

Wittenberg — Germany

W.K. & Co. — England

W.K.C. Co. — see 65.

W.L. over an L. — England

W.M. Co. — see 79., 94 (A.67,68)

Wolfe (& Hamilton) — England

two women on side of shield (N.J. Coat
  of Arms) — see 24., 30., 31., 36., 71.

two women (one seated) on sides of shield
  (N.Y. Coat of Arms) — see 57.

Wood (various) — England

Wooliscroft — England

Woolley — England

Worcester (Royal) — England

W.P.(ts.) Co. — see 78.

W.P.C. — see 77., 78.

W.P. Co. (as monogram with letters
  intertwined) — see 77.

W.P. Co. — see 55.

W.P.M. — Germany

W.P.P. Co. — see 61., 62.

W.Pts. Co. — see 78.

a wreath — see 27., 28., 30., 33., 45., 78.

a wreath with an anchor inside — see 14.

a wreath with a large circle inside —
  see 54.

a wreath with a crown inside — see 16.

a wreath with DRESDEN inside — see
  27., 28.

a wreath with an eagle inside — see
  88 (A.34)

a wreath with EMPIRE CHINA inside
  — see 83 (A.10)

a wreath with E.P.P. Co. monogram
  inside — see 30.

a wreath with a globe inside — see 19.

a wreath with HOTEL inside — see 74.

a wreath with a keystone inside — see 39.

a wreath with an L. inside — see 45.

a wreath with its ribbon on top — see 78.

a wreath with a shield inside — see 52.

a wreath with S.P. 1880 inside — see 33.

a wreath with T.P. Co. monogram inside
  — see 30.

a wreath with UNION CHINA inside
  — see 73.

a wreath with V.& B. monogram inside
  — see 74.

a wreath with a W. (as a fancy monogram)
  inside — see 78.

Wright, Russel — late U.S. (mostly
  1940s and 1950s)

W.R.S. & Co. — England

W.S. (& Co.) — England

W.S. & S. — Germany

W.S. George — see 33.

Wurttemberg — Germany

W.W. & Co. — England

Wyllie, H.R. — see 80.

Wyllie (,John,) & Son — see 79., 80.

Wyoming — see 42.

W.Y.S. — see 80.

Y. & B. — England

Yale — see 27., 42., 48.

Y.B.A. — see 22.

Z.B. (& S.) — England

Zell — Germany

Z.S. & Co. — Germany

Zsolnay — Hungary